Conserving the Commonwealth

CONSERVING THE COMMONWEALTH

The Early Years of the Environmental Movement in Virginia

Margaret T. Peters

Edited by Patricia Cecil Hass

With an afterword by FitzGerald Bemiss

University of Virginia Press   *Charlottesville and London*

University of Virginia Press
© 2008 by the Rector and Visitors of the University of Virginia
All rights reserved
Printed in the United States of America on acid-free paper

First published 2008

1 3 5 7 9 8 6 4 2

Library of Congress Cataloging-in-Publication Data
Peters, Margaret T.
    Conserving the Commonwealth : the early years of the environmental
movement in Virginia / Margaret T. Peters ; edited by Patricia Cecil Hass
with an afterword by FitzGerald Bemiss.
        p. cm.
    Includes bibliographical references and index.
    ISBN 978-0-8139-2773-2 (cloth : alk. paper)
    1. Environmentalism—Virginia—History. 2. Environmental
management—Virginia—History. 3. Conservation of natural resources—
Virginia—History. I. Hass, Patricia Cecil. II. Title.
    GE198.V8P48 2008
    333.7209755—dc22

2008012817

The paper used in this publication is Natures Natural,
produced without elemental chlorine compounds and blended with
acid-free pulps from non-old-growth forests.

Contents

In the spring of 2006 I was asked if I would be interested in working on a book with FitzGerald Bemiss on the environmental movement in Virginia since the mid-1960s. As a historian and a longtime staff member of the state's historic preservation office, I saw this as an opportunity to record a fascinating story involving men and women whom I had long admired and with many of whom I had worked during my tenure with the state.

From my earliest years with the Virginia Historic Landmarks Commission (now the Department of Historic Resources), FitzGerald Bemiss's name was always accorded the highest reverence—in my mind, he was acknowledged as the inspiration for the historic preservation and environmental movement in contemporary Virginia. Led by Bemiss, then a state senator, the Outdoor Recreation Study Commission produced *Virginia's Common Wealth,* a document that became a blueprint for nearly all of Virginia's subsequent environmental legislation, including the enabling legislation that created the Virginia Outdoors Foundation and the Virginia Historic Landmarks Commission, and called for the expansion of Virginia's state parks.

At the outset, I knew that because of serious time constraints the book could not be a completely comprehensive history of Virginia's environmental efforts since the 1960s—that is a task for another day— but it seemed imperative to record some of the highlights of the early days, and most especially the recollections of some of the key players. FitzGerald Bemiss had already assembled many of his thoughts, and several of his colleagues and friends—notably George Freeman, who was intimately involved with both land conservation and historic preservation, and the Honorable Tayloe Murphy, former member of the House of Delegates and former secretary of natural resources—had penned some of their recollections, and it was this body of work with which I began the task.

Over a period of six months I interviewed several dozen men and women, and without exception these dedicated individuals were more than generous with their time, their recollections, and their documents. Two former Virginia governors—A. Linwood Holton Jr. and Gerald L. Baliles—discussed their recollections of the origins of Virginia's environmental ethic. Conversations with A. E. Dick Howard, White Burkett Miller Professor of Law and Public Affairs at the University of Virginia, were inspiring. Howard had guided the writing of Virginia's 1971 constitution, which articulated for the first time the Commonwealth's responsibility to the environment. Michael Lipford, executive director of The Nature Conservancy in Virginia, provided most of the information relating to that critical land conservation organization in chapters 3 and 4. Dr. Junius R. Fishburne Jr., who served as the second director of the Virginia Historic Landmarks Commission, shared his insights on the historic preservation movement in Virginia and the role that Gerry Bemiss played in creating the state's first historic preservation agency. Leaders at the Department of Conservation, especially Joseph Maroon and Kathleen Kilpatrick at the Department of Historic Resources, were generous with their time and helped place the environmental movement in Virginia in its larger political context. Calder Loth, my former colleague at the Department of Historic Resources, who has faithfully shepherded the preservation easement program in Virginia for nearly three decades, shared his perspective on one of the most successful easement programs in the nation. Christopher Miller and Jolly deGive, president and director of planning services, respectively, for the Piedmont Environmental Council, supplied much information on that remarkable organization. Others who shared their comments and recollections include Tyson Van Auken, Clifford Schroeder, and Bob Lee for the Virginia Outdoors Foundation; Elizabeth Kostelny, executive director, and Louis Malon, director of preservation services, for the Association for the Preservation of Virginia Antiquities; Patricia Jackson, former director of the Lower James River Association; Dennis Baker, former director of state parks; Katherine Imhoff, vice president of the Thomas Jefferson Foundation and formerly executive director of the Population and Growth Commission (1991–95); Mrs. Robert Carter, who confirmed the significant role of the Garden Club of Virginia in its early commitment to preserving Virginia's priceless landscape resources; and Gerald McCarthy, longtime director of the Virginia Environmental Endowment, who provided a wonderful picture of the environmental landscape in the 1970s and '80s. Dr. John Moeser, author and professor emeritus of urban studies and planning at Virginia Commonwealth University and currently a visiting fellow at the University of Richmond, enlightened me about the serious issues of urbanization and urban sprawl, areas in which Gerry Bemiss has a long-standing interest. Garland "Trip" Pollard of the Southern Environmental Law Institute clarified many of the legal issues arising from conflicts over the environment and land conservation. Fred Fisher, a former assistant attorney general whose commitment to land conservation and historic preservation is well known, explained some of the critical court decisions on environmental issues. Tayloe Murphy spent half a day detailing his views about the political challenges involved in ensuring that Virginia's remarkable environmental resources will be here for future generations. Tayloe contributed substantially to chapter 7, which addresses his beloved Chesapeake Bay and the heroic efforts to save that priceless estuary.

Every effort was made to organize this book in a manner that would be as clear as possible to follow chronologically. In dealing with a number of subject areas, however—open space, historic buildings, water resources, parks, the Bay and rivers—it seemed best to address the early history of the environmental movement in Virginia (from 1966 to 1976) in the first two chapters, and then to consider what happened to those resources during the following decades in separate chapters.

Last and certainly not least, my deepest thanks go to George Freeman, whose years of dedicated service to the environmental community was reflected in his perseverance and skills in helping bring this project to a successful conclusion. George's knowledge of the inner workings of land conservation and open-space easements was invaluable in explaining and vividly illustrating the daunting challenges of preserving our shared heritage, addressed in chapter 4.

Beyond those I interviewed and those who contributed to the text, my sincerest appreciation goes to Patricia Cecil Hass, who brought to bear professional skills honed over many years as a senior editor at the publishing house of Alfred Knopf. Ms. Hass, a native Richmonder, has an abiding love for Virginia's landscape and resources, and her skill as an editor is matched only by her dedication to a cause in which she firmly believes. She has guided this effort in all of its many stages.

This effort would never have reached fruition without the inspiration of FitzGerald Bemiss, to whom I am grateful for the many hours of conversation and debate he gave to this work. As a lifelong environmentalist blessed with both the vision and the practical political skills to follow through on that vision, he has always been my hero. What a privilege it is to be able to tell this story, which so aptly reflects his dreams and struggles to ensure the future of Virginia's priceless and irreplaceable resources.

Margaret Peters
Richmond, Virginia
November 2007

The Historical Backdrop

THE COMMONWEALTH OF VIRGINIA is blessed with some of the most beautiful natural and historic resources in the nation. From the Tidewater in the east, with its stunning rivers and Chesapeake Bay, to the rolling Piedmont, dotted with historic towns, to the dramatic mountains, the Shenandoah Valley, and the southwestern highlands, Virginia can lay claim to as rich a landscape treasure as can be found anywhere in the world.

When John Smith arrived on the Virginia shores in 1607, he found a land of vast forests, tidal rivers filled with fish, oysters, and crabs, clear-running streams, and a landscape little touched except for limited cultivation of corn by a native population that showed considerable respect for the natural environment. Wildlife was abundant and the coastline pristine; there was no contamination of the waters or pollution of the air. Under the charter of the Virginia Company, the settlers were to take possession of "all the Lands, Woods, Soil, Grounds, Havens, Ports, Rivers, Mines, Minerals, Marshes, Waters, Fishings, Commodities," and to "dig mines and search for all Manner of Gold, Silver and Copper."[1] As far as they knew, the land they claimed stretched all the way to the Pacific Ocean, although they had no way of knowing where that was.

The settlers' awe of the wildlife and fish, forests, and endless land was tempered by the realities of survival—wide swings in summer and winter climate, hunger, disease, and sporadic Indian attacks. For the first thirty or forty years of the colony's existence, it was touch and go. But they did survive.

They built defensive shelters, cleared land, and learned from the Indians how to raise corn. They also developed discipline and political organization. They established parishes as their first political entities and built churches in them that functioned also as meeting places and courtrooms. New immigrants arrived, at first only replacing the large number of men who had died, mostly from disease and starvation. But eventually the colony began to grow and expand.

Economic success came with the cultivation of tobacco and its export to England. The local strain of tobacco was too harsh for English tastes, however, so in 1613 John Rolfe began growing a sweeter strain from Caribbean seeds. He traveled to London to develop a market, and by 1619 Virginia was exporting ten tons of tobacco to Europe each year. By 1639, with the help of the first Africans, who had arrived on a captured Dutch man-of-war in 1619, the colony was exporting 250 tons of tobacco a year.

Unlike the English colonies to the north, Virginia had few towns. There were plantation complexes, tiny courthouse villages, and later a few modest towns that thrived primarily because they were strategic shipping points. This dearth of towns persisted despite the Crown's efforts to get them established. The colony's legislative records are filled with such royal directives and charters. But the new towns usually failed or were so small as to be relatively insignificant. Urbanna, with a 1703 charter, was a survivor, while Hanovertown, north of Richmond, was not; only the ports were successful.

Modest changes in Virginia's countryside took place in the eighteenth century with the establishment of towns at the fall lines of the major rivers—Richmond on the James, Petersburg on the Appomattox, Fredericksburg on the Rappahannock, and Alexandria on the Potomac. The first passable roads were demanded by the farmers and agricultural interests, who needed to get their produce to market. The new roads often followed the natural traces of Indian trails. Travelers on horseback or in horse-drawn carts had to pay a fee to use these unpaved

Virginia's Counties and Independent Cities

0   12.5   25   50   75   100 Miles

VIRGINIA'S CITIES

Alexandria	1	Fredericksburg	14	Petersburg	27
Bedford	2	Galax	15	Poquoson	28
Bristol	3	Hampton	16	Portsmouth	29
Buena Vista	4	Harrisonburg	17	Radford	30
Charlottesville	5	Hopewell	18	Richmond	31
Chesapeake	6	Lexington	19	Roanoke	32
Colonial Heights	7	Lynchburg	20	Salem	33
Covington	8	Manassas	21	Staunton	34
Danville	9	Manassas Park	22	Suffolk	35
Emporia	10	Martinsville	23	Virginia Beach	36
Fairfax	11	Newport News	24	Waynesboro	37
Falls Church	12	Norfolk	25	Williamsburg	38
Franklin	13	Norton	26	Winchester	39

N

Lee, Scott, Wise 26, Dickenson, Buchanan, Russell, Washington 3, Tazewell, Smyth, Grayson, Carroll, Wythe, Bland, Pulaski, Giles, Montgomery 30, Floyd, Patrick, Henry 23, Franklin, Roanoke 33 32, Craig, Botetourt, Bedford 2, Pittsylvania 9, Halifax, Bath, Alleghany 8, Rockbridge 19 4, Amherst, Campbell, Charlotte, Mecklenburg, Brunswick, Lunenburg, Prince Edward, Appomattox 20, Buckingham, Cumberland, Nottoway, Amelia, Powhatan, Goochland, Fluvanna, Nelson, Albemarle 34, Augusta, Highland, Rockingham 17, Shenandoah, Page, Madison, Greene, Orange, Louisa, Hanover, Henrico 31, Chesterfield 7 18, Prince George 27, Dinwiddie, Sussex, Greensville 10, Southampton 13, Isle of Wight, Surry, James City 38, York 28 16, Charles City, New Kent, King William 24, King and Queen, Middlesex, Mathews, Gloucester, Lancaster, Richmond, Essex, King George, Caroline, Spotsylvania, Culpeper, Rappahannock, Fauquier 22, Prince William 21, Loudoun, Clarke, Frederick 39, Warren, Arlington 12, Fairfax 11, Stafford 14, Westmoreland, Northumberland, Accomack, Northampton, Buena Vista, Colonial Heights, Fredericksburg, Williamsburg, Poquoson, Hampton, Norfolk 25, Portsmouth 29, Virginia Beach 36, Chesapeake 6, Suffolk 35 "turnpikes" and "toll roads." County records of the early nineteenth century are filled with disputes about raising funds to build roads and applications to operate ferries to cross the innumerable waterways. The roads were few and far between, with little impact on the landscape, and most travel still took place by water.

Meanwhile, tobacco continued to be Virginia's "money crop," although wheat and other grains were gaining fast, particularly as settlement pushed into the northern and western parts of the state. In the early nineteenth century the James River and Kanawha Canal made Richmond a major U.S. port for the export of wheat to Europe.

By the 1830s the soil of the eastern part of the state had become depleted from overcultivation of tobacco, and many Virginia families moved westward, from Tidewater to the Southside and the Shenandoah Valley, and to other states to the west, leaving behind a declining population. Then some farsighted farmers initiated efforts to rejuvenate Virginia's agricultural economy. They banded together to establish agricultural societies that explored ways to replenish the soil on the farms, primarily by rotating crops. An early leader in this effort was General John Hartwell Cocke, who owned large plantations on the James below and above the fall line. Another was Edmund Ruffin of Hanover County, who experimented with "marling," using ground-up oyster shells to restore the soil. The efforts of these Virginia farmers to shift from tobacco to wheat and to use scientific agriculture represent the first awareness that Virginia's natural resources were not inexhaustible and that new methods were required to reverse the decline in the soil.

Before the American Civil War, large landholdings were the measure of a family's wealth, as were the slaves who enabled the cultivation of these vast acreages. The canals, and later the railroads, were built primarily to serve agriculture. In the immediate aftermath of the Civil War, the state was still largely agricultural, the landscape little changed.

The Tredegar Ironworks in Richmond became Virginia's first smokestack industry. After the war, Tredegar went back into business, producing iron rails and locomotives for the new railroads being built in Virginia and other southern states. Small towns began to thrive along repaired and newly constructed railroads. Railroads and coal mining fueled the growth of cities like Roanoke. The Shenandoah Valley towns—Lexington, Staunton, Harrisonburg, and Winchester—grew up along the old Valley Pike (U.S. Route 11) and became important markets for the region. Later in the nineteenth century the new steel industries of the Northeast needed Southwest Virginia's coal, and this led to the construction of major railroads from the mines to the ports of Hampton Roads.

Coal mining and widespread timbering caused real damage to Virginia's hillsides and streams. But, just as in the seventeenth century, Virginians viewed natural resources as unlimited and expressed little concern for conserving the landscape. The mining and timbering practices of those days did not earn good environmental marks. Few things are more destructive than an open slag pile leaching into a stream. Cutting timber along a ridge and down the slope is equally destructive, for it guarantees erosion and loss of ground cover. And where timber is cut and the residue left to rot, erosion and stream pollution follow.

As Virginia's cities grew, so did the demand for services. Recognizing the need for municipal water delivery systems, cities like Richmond, Charlottesville, Alexandria, Norfolk, and Fredericksburg developed waterworks, leading to concerns about the safety and purity of the water. But most Virginia citizens still drew their water from wells on their own property or shared with neighbors.

During the boom years of the early 1890s, those who could afford it fled the heat and humidity of lowland summers for the springs and spas in the mountains and the Valley. Entire towns were laid out, including Buena Vista in Rockbridge County and Paeonian Springs in Loudoun County. Part of their marketing strategy was the promotion of their healthful living environments and, in the case of Paeonian Springs, pure and healing spring water.

Construction of electric streetcars allowed easy access to the areas outside the downtowns, and many families chose to build in new suburbs, where they believed the environment would be better for their children. Even today one can see the sleeping porches built in that era;

sleeping in "fresh air" was considered good for children. Much of the impetus for the movement to the suburbs came from the new awareness of the importance of living in a healthful environment.

Streetcars also gave city dwellers access to surrounding parks. In Richmond, parks and recreation areas such as Westhampton Park (now part of the University of Richmond), Chimborazo, Byrd Park, and Forest Hill Park provided welcome respite from the city, and closer in, Monroe Park and the Fan District's triangle parks, easily accessible on foot, enabled even people who had no transportation to escape the city streets. Suburban villages like Ashland and Bon Air were easily reached by train, and Richmond residents often sought the fresh air and recreation opportunities available there.

From the 1890s to the 1920s, citizens continued to look for more varied lifestyles. Virginia had few cities from which a well-heeled citizenry sought escape, but the seeds had been planted for a philosophy that promoted so-called suburban living as a worthy goal. There also was growing scientific understanding of the threats to public health from crowded living conditions in communities with unsafe water and polluted air.

Meanwhile, the federal government began to recognize the need for conservation of the environment. National parks were created to protect America's great treasures: Wyoming's Yellowstone in 1872, California's Yosemite and Sequoia in 1890, and Washington's Mount Rainier in 1899. The 1906 Antiquities Act gave the president "authority to declare by public proclamation historic landmarks, historic and prehistoric structures, and other objects of scientific interest that are situated upon the lands owned or controlled by the Government of the United States to be national monuments."[2] In 1916, President Woodrow Wilson signed a bill creating the National Park Service as a separate bureau within the Department of the Interior. As early as 1908 Dr. J. Horace McFarland, one of the leaders in the creation of the Park Service, addressed a conference convened by President Theodore Roosevelt, saying, "The scenic value of all the national domain yet remaining should be jealously guarded as a distinctly important natural resource, and not as a mere incidental increment. In giving access for wise economic purposes to forest and range, to valley and stream, the Federal Government should not for a moment overlook the safeguarding to the people of all the natural beauty now existing. That this may be done without preventing legitimate use of all the other natural resources is certain."[3] McFarland thus articulated a national commitment to preserve open natural areas for public access, a philosophy that has survived to the present.

The first, and still the only, national park in Virginia is Shenandoah National Park, dedicated by President Franklin D. Roosevelt and opened in 1935, although its conception dated to the Calvin Coolidge administration.[4] It was the first national park in the eastern United States, and Virginia fought hard for this honor. Shenandoah National Park encompasses 197,000 acres, although its authorized size is larger. It includes the scenic Skyline Drive and the Appalachian Trail and contains more than five hundred miles of hiking trails, scenic views, and overlooks.[5]

The single late nineteenth-century invention that led to unparalleled change in the landscape was the automobile, which allowed people to travel long distances and resulted in demand for more and better roads and highways. Although the air pollution caused by many thousands of cars did not become a serious problem until later in the twentieth century, the construction of hundreds of miles of roadways radically altered the landscape and led ultimately to the sprawling suburban commercial and residential development we have today.

No one could have anticipated the degree to which Virginia's magnificent countryside would change by the mid-twentieth century. During the 1920s and 1930s, despite Harry F. Byrd's ambitious highway construction, most Virginians remained on the farm. Their way of life continued to be agricultural, and farmers were generally good stewards of the fields, and for the most part of the waterways, on which their livelihood depended. As Virginia recovered from the Great Depression, the agricultural economy revived, although small farmers found it difficult to compete with their larger neighbors.

With the onset of World War II, however, Virginia began to make the critical transition from a farm economy to a commercial and industrial-based way of life. Employment opportunities abounded in the urban areas. Large military installations in Northern Virginia, the Richmond area, Tidewater, and Southwest Virginia attracted thousands of workers to urban and suburban communities. The growing demand for housing led to the construction of planned developments. Although wartime housing construction did not approach the postwar level, new neighborhoods in urban areas like Norfolk and Arlington are even now old enough to be judged "historic."

The period following World War II was marked by tremendous growth, change, and development throughout the nation, and Virginia was no exception. Pent-up demand for housing exploded; hundreds of thousands of housing units were constructed. Owning a car, or even two cars, became commonplace. For the first time since the 1920s, people had money to spend. The GI Bill allowed returning soldiers access to higher education and thus to better-paying jobs. Massive unemployment was considered a thing of the past. Virginia was transformed, not only economically but physically and socially as well.

This postwar explosion of growth and development caught Virginia unawares. In a state whose rural and agricultural traditions were taken for granted, few people thought that the Commonwealth should take steps to protect natural areas for the benefit of the public. But, providentially, the state was fortunate to have a remarkable group of farsighted leaders who shared a love of the natural world and the vision to sense danger, and who would provide Virginia with the means to preserve her environmental heritage. These dedicated men and women would devote their energy and commitment to open-space protection, parkland acquisition, historic preservation, and thoughtful governmental regulation. Their inspiring example reminds us that although Virginia's natural environment has suffered huge losses over the years, new efforts can be mounted that will inspire future generations.

The state can yet save itself from destruction.

The Vision and the Beginning

O N OCTOBER 12, 1960, a seminal meeting took place in the living room of Elizabeth Scott Bocock (Mrs. John H. Bocock) at 909 West Franklin Street in Richmond. The Virginia chapter of The Nature Conservancy was born at this meeting, and in attendance were two young men who were to become the first leaders in Virginia's environmental movement—Virginia state senator FitzGerald (Gerry) Bemiss and attorney George Clemon Freeman Jr. Also at the meeting was Richard Pough, then president of The Nature Conservancy.[1] Four years later Bemiss and Freeman would work together to craft the landmark Virginia Outdoors Plan, the first significant legislative effort to protect the state's environment.

FitzGerald Bemiss grew up on Monument Avenue in Richmond, "eyeball to eyeball with Traveller" from his third-floor bedroom, as he expressed it. His happiest childhood memories were of long hours spent at Brookbury, his grandmother's farm in Chesterfield County, in what was then deep country and is now built-up suburbia. Cherished memories of running free in the Virginia woods and countryside led to his love and respect for open spaces as worthy of care and conservation. As an adult, Bemiss joined his father's business, the Virginia Skyline Company, which won the contract to provide the visitor services in Shenandoah National Park. Bemiss was elected to the Virginia House of Delegates in 1955 as a businessman, one of the few nonlawyers in the General Assembly. His credentials as a Byrd Democrat won him the plum assignment of a seat on the Appropriations Committee during his terms in the House. In 1960, Bemiss was elected to the Virginia Senate.

George Freeman, an Alabama native, had been a brilliant law student and had clerked for Supreme Court Justice Hugo Black before joining the firm of Hunton & Williams in Richmond, where Lewis F. Powell Jr. was a partner. Powell later took Black's place as an associate justice on the Supreme Court. Freeman was on his way to becoming a leading attorney in the field of land conservation.

The Commonwealth's environmental movement was officially born on March 31, 1964, when the Virginia General Assembly adopted a resolution that created the Virginia Outdoor Recreation Study Commission (VORSC). Governor Albertis Harrison appointed FitzGerald Bemiss to chair the new VORSC,[2] and George Freeman served as its special counsel.

Today, the term "outdoor recreation" sounds quaint, a relic of the early days of Virginia's urbanization. In the mid-twentieth century the term referred to the appreciation of natural beauty and recreational opportunities. Over time environmental terminology has changed to reflect our increased knowledge and shifting environmental challenges. Yet the General Assembly's 1964 resolution defined the issues with which the state still grapples forty-odd years later. The act's introduction reads in part:

> Whereas, there is constantly increasing demand for outdoor recreation facilities and constantly decreasing open space for providing these facilities; and
>
> Whereas, Virginia's population is increasing rapidly and becoming overcrowded in urban and suburban areas; and
>
> Whereas the Commonwealth has no comprehensive policy or plan for meeting present and anticipated needs for outdoor recreation; and
>
> Whereas it is recognized that adequate outdoor recreation facilities are vital to Virginia's general happiness and social and economic development.[3]

Bemiss knew that he needed a vice chair for the VORSC who could effectively secure political support in the General Assembly for VORSC recommendations. Bemiss himself was somewhat "out of the loop," having opposed the doctrine of Massive Resistance earlier, and thus was regarded by older Byrd stalwarts in the Virginia Senate with deep apprehension. So he asked Governor Harrison to appoint then state senator Harry F. Byrd Jr., whose congeniality, political acumen, and influence would be invaluable. He also proposed the appointment of two nationally respected warriors in the field, Conrad Wirth, director of the National Park Service, and Ira Gabrielson, retired director of the National Fish and Wildlife Service. Both men brought with them years of experience in conservation and park management.[4]

The VORSC was inspired in part by work done several years earlier by the National Outdoor Recreation Resources Review Commission, chaired by Laurance Rockefeller, an ardent conservationist. Among the Rockefeller Commission members was Henry L. Diamond, who had led the New York State Park and Natural Areas Program and was one of Rockefeller's associates in his efforts to conserve the environment. Another commission member was William H. Whyte, the noted author of *The Organization Man* (1956). His 1959 study, *Conservation Easements,* led to the enactment of open-space legislation in California, New York, Connecticut, and Massachusetts.

The VORSC could have had no better national model than the Rockefeller Commission and its 1962 report, which "urged all levels of government and the private sector to come up with the money to meet the needs it found."[5] Following the example of the Rockefeller Commission, the VORSC broadened its mandate from the beginning, setting up advisory committees to study seven important issues: historic preservation, floodplain zoning, local authority, impounded waters, travel, public relations, and land taxation and zoning. Most of the members of these advisory committees were not VORSC members but rather concerned citizens knowledgeable in their particular fields.

At its organizational meeting in September 1964, the VORSC planned a series of five public hearings around the state to present its proposals to Virginia citizens and solicit their ideas. Bemiss believed that these hearings would offer commission members the opportunity to "see firsthand" the various geographic areas of the state.

The public hearings evoked an enthusiastic response, a measure of the citizenry's awakening concern about the environment. A number of groups called for the state to take a more active role, and many suggested the creation of a central planning agency for natural resources. Local governments asked for more technical planning assistance from the state. Extensive coverage in the Richmond newspapers reflected the growing interest in the VORSC's progress. One news report quoted from a presentation made by commission member Ira Gabrielson, which called for the preservation of Virginia's coastal marshes: "The Virginia marshes, particularly those of the Eastern Shore, are of prime importance to the waterfowl of the entire Atlantic coast, and their value will increase and grow as the years go by."[6]

Testimony by Richard D. Chumney, commissioner of agriculture, clarified that the number of acres in public ownership that might be used for recreational purposes was not an issue; the question was where to locate recreational facilities and how to address the lack of local land-use management. He said Virginians needed a better understanding of land-use planning and zoning to ensure the attractive development of open spaces. Bemiss, speaking to the Virginia Nurserymen's Association, agreed, but added, "Virginians must conserve these open spaces before encroaching development leaves the state barren of adequate recreational facilities. . . . This is the first generation of Virginians to come along who cannot take open spaces for granted."[7]

The work of the VORSC advisory committees produced far-reaching results. The most immediately successful was the Committee on Historic Preservation. Its members were Edward P. Alexander, vice president of Colonial Williamsburg; Randolph W. Church, Librarian of Virginia; Elbert Cox, regional director of the National Park Service, Southeast Region; John Melville Jennings, director of the Virginia Historical Society; Frederick D. Nichols, professor of architecture at the University of Virginia; and Charles C. Wall, resident director of Mount Vernon. They took the ball and ran with it, and their work resulted in the creation of the Virginia Historic Landmarks Commission.[8]

The VORSC advisory committee charged with examining the question of local authority, however, faced serious obstacles. Speaking in Washington in 1965, Senator Bemiss articulated the issues:

> The new phenomenon of the metropolitan area, or megalopolis, creates
> a problem with which the present shape and authority of local govern-
> ments cannot cope. The core of the problem is the complete economic,
> social and physical interdependence of the urban metropolitan area's
> components versus traditional illusions and mechanisms of sovereign
> independence. . . . The resulting costly stalemate is only dealt with when
> two or more localities are sufficiently compelled by either a common
> problem . . . or a common resource to create a regional planning commis-
> sion to think about the joint concern.[9]

In the same speech, Bemiss called for localities to work cooperatively to meet the open-space and outdoor recreation needs of their citizens.

In 1965, as the VORSC labored on its report, its members took to the hustings to promote and publicize its work, preparing the ground for the presentation of the report to the General Assembly. A column by Charles Houston in the *Richmond News Leader* reported that "the Commission is interested in getting open spaces set aside for the use of Virginians before there are no open spaces left."[10]

Bemiss addressed the Richmond Council of Women's Organizations, expressing his appreciation for the important role of women's groups in the environmental field and in providing political support for the recommendations of the VORSC. He also spoke to the Associated Clubs of Virginia for Roadside Development, which included the Garden Club of Virginia, the Virginia Federation of Women's Clubs, the Virginia Federation of Garden Clubs, and the Virginia Federation of Home Demonstration Clubs. In this speech he bemoaned the fact that in all the millions spent on new highways, there had been little concern for their scenic beauty. "Some roads in Virginia do not need money," he said, "but need protection to keep them in their present state." The Federal Bureau of Public Roads and Virginia's own Highway Department "should engineer roads in a way that respects the landscape they go through."[11] Bemiss's vision anticipated by several years federal legislation mandating that the landscape and environment be considered in planning new primary roads and interstate highways.[12] Also in 1965, the governor appointed Bemiss to chair a special legislative committee on water resources to coordinate efforts for the conservation of water and the development of the state's river basins.[13]

While the work of the VORSC progressed, a significant event took place in Washington that would have an impact on the future of Virginia's environmental movement. In February 1965, President Lyndon B. Johnson delivered a message to Congress in which he said, "For centuries Americans have drawn strength and inspiration from the beauty of our country. It would be a neglectful generation indeed, indifferent alike to the judgment of history and the command of principle, which failed to preserve and extend such a heritage for its descendants. Yet the storm of modern change is threatening to blight and diminish in a few decades what has been cherished and protected for generations. A growing population is swallowing up areas of natural beauty with its demands for living space, and is placing increased demands on our overburdened areas of recreation and pleasure."[14]

Thus was born the "Beauty for America" White House Conference, which assembled conservationists, political leaders, preservationists, planners, architects, and scientists from across the nation. President Johnson appointed Laurance Rockefeller to chair the conference. Rockefeller effectively explained the mission to a public that he assumed was skeptical about political leaders spending their time "talking about beauty." As Rockefeller explained later, "the President, the leaders, and most significantly, the people of this country have become concerned about the kind of America our affluence is creating. . . . In many ways, natural beauty is an inadequate term for this concern. . . . What is involved here is the basic quality of the environment—the health of the land and water and air on which man depends for life, as do all living things."[15]

Governor Harrison asked Bemiss to represent Virginia at the White House Conference, and Rockefeller selected him to chair a panel on the "new suburbia," one of the subjects most germane to the environmental challenges in Virginia. Bemiss's comments, both in his introduction to the panel's report to the conference and in the text itself, could have been written today. Years later, Rockefeller praised Bemiss's contribution in glowing terms. "One of the major goals of the White House Conference on Natural Beauty and the Outdoor Recreation Resources Review Commission was to stimulate efforts in the various states. I remember well your leadership in Virginia as one of the first states to respond to our recommendations. You certainly made an outstanding contribution to the well being of Virginians. . . . Achieving balance between public access and use and conservation of natural values has been a theme of our work through the years, and I know from your combination of business, legal and conservation careers, you have contributed to this concept."[16]

Bemiss recalled an encounter at the conference with President Johnson, who looked him squarely in the eye and declared that he wanted the cooperation of all the states—not forty-seven or forty-eight but all fifty.[17] With this exhortation in mind, Bemiss returned to Richmond and his VORSC responsibilities. The contagious excitement of the White House Conference spilled over into the work of the Virginians as they went about their task.

The VORSC finished its report in the fall of 1965, presenting it to the General Assembly on November 1. Bemiss came up with its title: *Virginia's Common Wealth.*[18] The report presented the results of the VORSC's study of Virginia's outdoor recreation resources, as well as the commission's Virginia Outdoors Plan—twenty-one specific recommendations for conserving and developing Virginia's outdoor recreation resources for the lasting public benefit. The report also proposed eight bills for the consideration of the General Assembly.

The Virginia Outdoors Plan articulated an environmental philosophy and held that it was incumbent upon a responsible citizenry to protect the cleanliness of its air and water, preserve its historic buildings and sites, and take care of its open spaces, woodlands, rivers, parks, and recreation areas. The plan still serves as a blueprint for Virginia's environmental stewards, as pertinent today as it was then.

The VORSC's major findings were that

- *There is a strong and growing demand for more outdoor recreation opportunities.* The population is increasing dramatically. Not only are there more and more Virginians, increasingly they are living closer and closer together. Yet they have more leisure time than ever before, they have higher incomes, and they have more automobiles. These are the dynamic factors behind Virginians' demand for more access to the Virginia outdoors and for places to walk, to swim, to launch a boat, to camp—to loaf and recreate themselves.

- *Existing facilities are inadequate for present demands.* This is true in all resource categories—from high-density neighborhood parks to remote natural areas. There is a serious deficiency in number, location, and variety of State Parks.

- *The need for action is most urgent in metropolitan areas.* Three-fourths of Virginia's population will soon live in these areas. Meanwhile open space for outdoor recreation is being consumed, spoiled, or made unavailable at an alarming rate.

- *The term "outdoor recreation" must include the entire Virginia outdoor environment.* Outdoor recreation must involve State Parks and the roads which take people to them; municipal parks and playgrounds and habitable communities; access to ample, unpolluted water; historical sites and harmonious countryside. All of these are outdoor recreation resources and they must be dealt with as interrelated parts of the total environment in which Virginians work, play, and live.

- *Each individual, and his government at all levels—local, regional, state, and federal—has a job to do.* Individuals, non-governmental organizations, and private enterprise are providing many outstanding recreation opportunities. Virginia has benefited greatly from broad individual concern for the Virginia landscape. Garden clubs, conservation organizations, non-profit historical preservation corporations, service clubs, and others like them should be aided and encouraged by the state in every possible way. The state should also encourage private enterprise and the travel industry to develop outdoor recreation facilities and to provide the services needed in support of public facilities.

Even as *Virginia's Common Wealth* emphasized local responsibility for the establishment of parks and recreation facilities, and for the protection of significant environmental resources, it was unequivocal in its call for regional planning and action when two or more localities shared a common resource. It laid responsibility upon the state for overall coordination and leadership, conservation of natural resources, and establishment of an "adequate system of State Parks and Recreation Areas to meet statewide needs beyond the responsibility and capacity of local and regional agencies." It called upon the state to "offer planning and financial aid to local and regional agencies for land acquisition" and to "raise a high standard. A basic condition of financial aid should be basic land use planning and conservation zoning by the locality." The report also recommended that the state coordinate its programs with those of federal agencies and "maintain a comprehensive plan for sharing in the Federal Land and Water Conservation Fund."

Virginia's Common Wealth showed amazing prescience in its recommendations concerning water resources and river basins: "It is increasingly clear that the present demands on Virginia's rivers—their waters and their shorelines—require comprehensive river basin research and planning to conserve our most vital resources." In addition, the VORSC was well aware that pollution in the Chesapeake Bay came from the rivers that emptied directly into it, and from the watersheds of the state's larger rivers, which drain the majority of the state.

The VORSC report concluded, "The State must look ahead. Critical challenges of urbanization and industrialization demand new and advanced thinking. The State must take the leadership now in a plan of action—the Virginia Outdoors Plan."

The eight bills in the legislative package, which George Freeman helped to craft, were the following:

1. *The Open Space Land Act:* A bill to provide for the acquisition and designation of real property by certain public bodies for use as permanent open-space land, and to that end to confer certain powers upon such public bodies, and to permit them to exercise the power of eminent domain, appropriate funds, levy taxes and assessments, and issue bonds; prescribe conditions under which such property may be diverted to other purposes, and be conveyed or leased; and provide for exemption of such property from taxation. It also provided that:

   > No open-space land, the title to or interest or right in which has been acquired under this act or which has been designated as open-space under the authority of this act, shall be converted or diverted from open-space land use unless the conversion or diversion is determined by the public body to be (1) essential to the orderly development and growth of the urban area, and (2) in accordance with the official comprehensive plan for the urban area in effect at the time of conversion or diversion. Other real property of at least equal fair market value and of nearly as feasible equivalent usefulness and location for use as permanent open-space land shall be substituted within a reasonable period not exceeding one year for any real property converted or diverted from open-space land use, unless the public body should determine that such open-space land or its equivalent is no longer needed. The public body shall assure that the property substituted will be subject to the provisions of this act.

2. *A Commission of Outdoor Recreation:* A bill to create the Commission of Outdoor Recreation; provide for the appointment, qualifications, terms of office, and compensation of members thereof; provide for the employment of certain agents and employees; prescribe certain powers and duties of the Commission; require departments, commissions, boards, agencies, officers, and institutions of the state government and political subdivisions thereof to cooperate with the

Commission in certain respects; give the force and effect of law to certain rules and provide a penalty for violation thereof; prescribe the procedure for the exercise of the power of eminent domain; appropriate funds to the Commission; and repeal certain acts.

3. *Zoning Enabling Law Amendments:* A bill to amend and reenact [certain provisions] of the Code of Virginia relating to planning, subdivision of land, and zoning so as to define open space and enable counties and municipalities to enact ordinances in reference thereto.

4. *A Scenic Highway and Historic Road System:* A bill to amend the Code of Virginia . . . , authorizing the State Highway Commission to designate highways in a certain manner under certain conditions; defining certain terms; conferring upon the State Highway Commissioner additional powers of eminent domain; and to appropriate funds.

5. *Access Roads to Recreation Areas:* A bill to amend the Code of Virginia by adding a section . . . providing for the setting aside of certain funds; authorizing the State Highway Commissioner to construct, reconstruct, maintain, or improve certain roads upon certain conditions; making such roads part of certain highway systems; permitting certain State agencies to make regulations; and to appropriate funds.

6. *A Historic Landmarks Commission:* A bill to create the Virginia Historic Landmarks Commission to provide for the appointment of the members thereof; to prescribe the powers and duties of the Commission with reference to the establishment, designation, preservation, and marking of historic landmarks and historic districts; to prescribe the effect of assessment for taxation of designation of historic landmarks and historic districts; to empower the Commission, under certain conditions, to acquire property by purchase or condemnation; to transfer to the Commission certain powers and duties with respect to historic markers; and to appropriate funds.

7. *The Virginia Outdoors Foundation:* A bill to create the Virginia Outdoors Foundation and governing body, prescribe its powers and
   functions, and appropriate money therefor.

8. *Virginia Park Revenue Bond Act Amendment:* A bill to amend and
   reenact [certain sections] of the Code of Virginia relating to issuance
   of revenue bonds for camping and recreational facilities and fees
   and charges in connection therewith.

Newspaper support for the Virginia Outdoors Plan legislation package was immediate and enthusiastic. On November 7, 1965, the *Richmond Times-Dispatch* gave it front-page coverage as well as editorial
endorsement.[19] The same day, the *Roanoke Times* described the plan as
"an exciting, comprehensive and absolutely essential program for conserving and developing the State's water and land resources for present
day Virginians and future generations."[20]

Inspired by the White House Conference, Governor Harrison called
for a comparable gathering in Virginia to promote the VORSC findings. The Virginia Conference on Natural Beauty was convened at the
John Marshall Hotel in Richmond on December 9, 1965, and was
attended by more than a thousand people. It was chaired by Carlisle
Humelsine, president of Colonial Williamsburg. Governor Harrison's
opening address was a clarion call for conservation: "The aim of the
Virginia conference will be to emphasize the need to protect and preserve what is historically significant and esthetically pleasing and to
insure that what we build in years to come will enhance rather than
detract from the beauty of Virginia."[21] The governor pointed to *Virginia's Common Wealth* as a blueprint for what needed to be done,
region by region. William H. Whyte and FitzGerald Bemiss also spoke,
and the Colonial Williamsburg Foundation produced a film for the
conference called *Virginia's Beauty Crisis.*

In the following month, January 1966, Bemiss presented the VORSC
legislative package to the Virginia General Assembly. All eight bills
were passed, and the Virginia Outdoors Plan was enacted into law.

It is worth reiterating that although Virginia's initial efforts were a
response to federal leadership, after the publication of *Virginia's Com-*

State Senator FitzGerald Bemiss (second from left), accompanied by Senators
William B. Spong Jr. (far left) and Harry Byrd Jr. (center) and Elbert Cox, director of
the Virginia Commission of Outdoor Recreation (far right), accepting a Land and
Water Conservation Fund grant on behalf of Governor Mills Godwin from Secretary
of the Interior Stewart Udall (second from right), August 9, 1967. For discussion, see
chapter 3, page 23. (U.S. Department of the Interior)

mon Wealth the tables were turned. Virginia enacted its environmental
legislation before the federal government created the U.S. Environmental Protection Agency (EPA) and enacted the National Environmental Policy Act in the late 1960s.

George Freeman saw his principal contribution to the Virginia legislative package as the provision in the Open Space Land Act that
created the state's "perpetual open-space easement" program. Some
Virginia lawyers had doubted that easements could be used for conservation purposes, but Freeman prevailed.[22]

Years later, FitzGerald Bemiss discussed what he had sought to
accomplish in the work of the VORSC. "We wanted Virginians to know
they had a clear and forceful mandate," he recalled, "for the steps recommended in the Report. Our natural resources are gifts we must care
for. We wanted to arouse a conservation conscience." When asked

about the VORSC's greatest accomplishments, he replied, "The first big accomplishment was securing funds from the federal Land and Water Fund to begin the efforts to expand Virginia's state park system; the second was the establishment of the earliest and best easement program in the nation; and the third was the establishment and growth of the Virginia Historic Landmarks Commission."[23]

From today's perspective, the primary accomplishment of this 1966 legislation was to open the eyes of Virginians, who for centuries had taken for granted their exceptional natural and historic resources. Some forty years later, we still have the means to preserve our Virginia heritage, but the problems have worsened, and the efforts it will now take to save and expand it have grown more difficult and expensive. We have celebrated the four-hundredth anniversary of the landing at Jamestown, and John Smith's seventeenth-century description of the pristine Bay and its tributaries is an eloquent reminder of the damage we have done and the work for preservation we still must do if we are to save Virginia for our children and their children's children.

Milestones, 1966–1976

THE NEW LAWS of the Virginia Outdoors Plan came into effect in July 1966,[1] and then began what has been called the "golden age of environmental leadership in Virginia."[2] FitzGerald Bemiss prevailed upon Elbert Cox to take on the newly created position of director of the Virginia Commission on Outdoor Recreation, a victory that Bemiss later viewed as one of his own great triumphs.[3] Cox, one of the most experienced and valuable members of the VORSC, chose to leave a senior post in the National Park Service to launch the fledgling commission. He went right to work. In August 1966 he proposed that the state appropriate $3.5 million to acquire land and improve Virginia's state parks. This was the first action taken on behalf of the Virginia Outdoors Plan; in the winter of 1967 the Virginia legislature appropriated the funds.[4]

With the appropriation of the state funds, Virginia qualified for a $1,663,000 grant from the federal Land and Water Conservation Fund, established in 1964 to assist states that developed long-range plans for outdoor recreation.[5] Bemiss and Cox traveled to Washington on behalf of Governor Godwin to accept Virginia's first federal grant of $500,000. Stewart L. Udall, secretary of the interior, presented the check to them at a ceremony attended by Virginia's senators, Harry F. Byrd Jr. and William B. Spong Jr., both of whom had served with Bemiss in the Virginia Senate. Harry Byrd, before being appointed to finish his father's term in Washington, had been the effective vice chair of the VORSC. The federal money, along with $750,000 in state funds, was used to acquire the land for Mason Neck State Park, adjacent to the site of George Mason's Gunston Hall, and False Cape State Park in Virginia Beach, and to help with some regional parks, among them the James River Park in Richmond.[6]

Another magnificent piece of land on the Potomac River was saved in a more roundabout manner. The VORSC report, *Virginia's Common Wealth,* had divided the state into ten regions within which desirable park locations were indicated but left purposely unnamed. This was because there had been no study of any of the sites or alternatives, and the VORSC had been anxious not to stir up any objections. Unfortunately, however, one of its desired park locations was labeled "Smoot Farm." This was a property called Caledon owned by Ann Hopewell Smoot. As Bemiss later recounted:

At a cousin's wedding in Rapidan in the summer I was startled to be introduced to Mrs. Smoot, who gave me a real dressing down about leaving her farm's name in the report. I could only say that the error was entirely my fault and apologized. I then spent most of the afternoon chatting pleasantly with Mrs. Smoot. When she left, I saw her to her car and said, "Mrs. Smoot, I don't want to sail under false colors. I am bound to tell you that we would love to have Caledon as a State Park." Mrs. Smoot laughed and departed.

A few weeks later, she telephoned and said, "I want to give you the farm, but for goodness sakes don't say anything about it until I clear it with Judge Smith." Her lawyer, Howard Smith, was chairman of the House Rules Committee in Congress. In those days, every bill came through his committee, where, without his approval, it stayed. He had been known to stop the wheels of government by sitting on his front porch and refusing to go to town. In this case he objected to Mrs. Smoot's gift, and she asked to be released from her commitment. I agreed immediately, saying she had been nothing but generous, and I understood the situation entirely. Then she said, "Don't give up. I'll work on the judge." In about two weeks she called again. She had cleared it with the judge and wanted to give the state of Virginia two thousand open acres and four miles of Potomac shoreline. Caledon is now a "state park natural area" protecting nesting grounds of the American eagle.[7]

The VORSC knew it needed to tackle the problems of Virginia's metropolitan areas, which were specifically mentioned in *Virginia's Common Wealth,* although no legislation was proposed on the subject. Virginia's population had grown exponentially. The state's population first reached one million in 1830, and the second million was not achieved until 1910. The third million came in 1945, and in 1960 the population was four million. By 2005 there were some 7.5 million Virginians. The population in Northern Virginia alone grew by an astronomical 34 percent between 1980 and 1990, with 94 percent of that increase in the so-called outlying counties of Prince William, Spotsylvania, and Stafford. A formerly rural area such as Loudoun County

Ann Hopewell Smoot, with State Senator FitzGerald Bemiss, Judge Howard Smith, and Governor Mills Godwin. (Mr. and Mrs. FitzGerald Bemiss)

sustained a population of fewer than fifty-eight thousand in 1980 but had grown by more than 50 percent by 1990.[8] At the same time, rural areas like Southside, Southwest Virginia, and Appalachia, and urban centers like Richmond, Norfolk, and Fairfax City were ceding large numbers of residents to exurbia and the new urban counties encircling diminishing population centers.

Virginia's major metropolitan areas were and are typically composed of separate political entities—counties, cities, and towns, each with its own governing body. This system of political subdivision—unique to Virginia—is a major obstacle to sensible land-use planning and historical and open-space preservation. The Richmond metropolitan region, for example, was made up of a core city, two urban counties (Henrico and Chesterfield), and four rural but rapidly urbanizing counties (New Kent, Hanover, Goochland, and Powhatan). Technically and politically cut up into separate governmental subdivisions, Richmond is economically and culturally one unit with many interdependent parts. Air pollution, traffic congestion, insufficient water supply, and inadequate recreation areas are all regional problems that do not respect political boundaries.

Virginia's Common Wealth advocated local and regional planning, land acquisition of threatened areas and historic landmarks, and limits on unfettered development, as "three basic ways in which the State can help localities in meeting their share of the total Virginia Outdoors Plan." Unfortunately, in the intervening decades, localities have not gotten the state assistance they need to address their environmental problems.

At the 1966 session of the General Assembly, Governor Godwin asked the legislature to authorize a new Metropolitan Areas Study Commission to address the problems of Virginia's metropolitan areas. This body became known as the Hahn Commission after its chair, T. Marshall Hahn, president of Virginia Tech, and FitzGerald Bemiss served as a member.

Among his efforts on the Hahn Commission, Bemiss tried to get support for merging two or three counties within a metropolitan area into one political unit and then merging that with its metropolitan core city. Bemiss could already foresee the dire ramifications of urban sprawl. The urban county was a new and powerful concept to which the state had paid little attention. Such reorganization would improve services and reduce costs throughout the united metropolitan area.

The Hahn Commission's report, published in 1967, found that "much of the state's growth during the past several decades has occurred in its urban areas, a trend that will intensify in the years ahead. . . . If Virginians are to enjoy maximum opportunities for economic advancement and the most beneficial environment, then positive constructive steps to deal more effectively with the problems of the metropolitan areas are essential."[9]

The Hahn report went on to identify the most serious problems facing metropolitan areas, but it failed to recommend the obvious overall solution Bemiss had proposed: reduce the number of counties in Virginia and consolidate cities and the surrounding urban and urbanizing counties into "metropolitan regions." Such reorganization would have ensured that comprehensive and coordinated land-use planning and delivery of services were required at a regional level. But historical tradition, local political jealousy, and lingering racism made this bold suggestion politically impractical. In its place, therefore, the Hahn report proposed a halfway solution: regional "planning districts," with an option for localities to step up to more formalized "service districts" to accomplish local government cooperation. The Hahn report stopped short of requiring localities to participate. Accepting another layer of bureaucracy as the only politically palatable solution, the General Assembly enacted this legislation in its 1968 session.[10]

The next milestone in the history of Virginia's efforts to protect its environment came in 1968, when a blue-ribbon panel—the Commission on Constitutional Revision—was charged with rewriting the 1902 state constitution. The immediate impetus was the need to issue bonds to create the community college system proposed by Governor Godwin. Former governor Albertis Harrison was appointed commission chair, and A. E. Dick Howard, a professor of law at the University of Virginia, became its executive director.[11] Howard was a committed environmentalist who, along with Dennis Barnes, an associate professor of environmental sciences, had developed one of the first environmental law courses in the nation.[12] Howard also was a Rhodes Scholar and former law clerk to U.S. Supreme Court Justice Hugo Black.[13]

Virginia's 1902 constitution mentioned only one environmental imperative: the preservation of oyster beds in the Chesapeake Bay. But the framers of the new constitution recognized the need to address broader environmental and historic preservation issues introduced by the VORSC, as well as questions that had arisen in the wake of the 1966 Virginia Outdoors Plan legislation. They proposed new language "in recognition of the growing awareness that among the fundamental problems which will confront the Commonwealth in the coming years will be those of the environment."[14]

The language in the initial draft of the proposed new state constitution for Article XI, conservation, sections 1 and 2, was hortatory rather than mandatory. Conservationists and environmentalists knew that this language would not guarantee positive state action. Delegate Clive Duval of Northern Virginia, who had taken up the environmental cause in the legislature, advocated far stronger language, arguing, "people have a *right* to clean air and water and to the use and enjoyment for recreation of adequate public lands, waters and other natural resources."[15] The commission and the legislators rejected Duval's wording, but the final language in sections 1 and 2 of Article XI made it clear that protecting the environment was henceforth to be state policy. As ratified, those sections of the 1970 constitution read:

Section 1. Lands and resources of the Commonwealth.

To the end that the people have clean air, pure water, and the use and enjoyment for recreation of adequate public lands, waters, and other natural resources, it *shall be the policy of the Commonwealth* to conserve, develop, and utilize its natural resources, its public lands, and its historical sites and buildings. Further, it shall be the Commonwealth's policy to protect its atmosphere, lands, and waters from pollution, impairment, or destruction, for the benefit, enjoyment, and general welfare of the people of the Commonwealth.

Section 2. Conservation and development of natural resources and historical sites.

In the furtherance of such policy, the General Assembly may undertake the conservation, development, or utilization of lands or natural resources of the Commonwealth, the acquisition and protection of historical sites and buildings, and the protection of its atmosphere, lands, and waters from pollution, impairment, or destruction, by agencies of the Commonwealth or by the creation of public authorities, or by leases or other contracts with agencies of the United States, with other states, with units of government in the Commonwealth, or with private persons or corporations. Notwithstanding the time limitations of the provisions of Article X, Section 7, of this constitution, the Commonwealth may participate for any period of years in the cost of projects which shall be the subject of a joint undertaking between the Commonwealth and any agency of the United States or of other states. (Emphasis added.)

There was no precedent in Virginia's constitutional history for the new constitution's sweeping statement of a state environmental policy.[16] George Freeman advised his senior partner, Lewis Powell, a member of the Commission on Constitutional Revision, that the new language would conclusively counter any future argument against the use of conservation easements for historic and open-space preservation conveyed after the 1966 Virginia Outdoors Plan laws. This conclusion was validated years later by a 2005 Virginia Supreme Court decision upholding the validity of a perpetual conservation easement conveyed to a private charity between 1966 and 1988. The framers of the new constitution also proposed repeal of the "equal taxation" provision in the old 1902 constitution, which barred land-use taxation.[17]

In January 1970, Linwood Holton was sworn in as governor. His inaugural address stressed two priorities for his administration: protection of the environment and race relations.[18] Governor Holton had a more comprehensive agenda than had most Virginia environmental advocates in the past, whose primary focus was conservation of open space and creation of recreational areas. During Holton's term momentum broadened to encompass the protection of basic resources like air and water and the abatement of pollution.

On April 22, 1970, Governor Holton joined in Virginia's celebration of the first Earth Day. Some environmentalists suggest that Earth Day 1970 was a watershed event across the nation as well as in Virginia. Organized by students at Virginia Commonwealth University, the celebration was held in Richmond's historic Monroe Park. Holton recalls that some of his aides questioned his participation in Earth Day ceremonies, but he went anyway, finding among the young participants a high level of constructive and contagious excitement.[19]

The contagion seems to have been widespread. The electorate supported the revised constitution by better than a 70 percent margin in November 1970. This was proof of broad public support both for an environmental ethic as state policy and for recognition of the Commonwealth's responsibility for the care and protection of its natural resources.

One of Governor Holton's close allies and advisors was John W. Hanes Jr., a former U.S. assistant secretary of state under John Foster Dulles. Hanes, who lived in Great Falls, was active in efforts to conserve land and historic view sheds along the Potomac and was deeply involved in the conservation efforts of The Nature Conservancy in Northern Virginia as chairman of its Virginia chapter. He and Gerry Bemiss were instrumental in persuading Governor Holton to create a Council on the Environment by executive order. Bemiss recalls that the governor chortled with delight as he told Bemiss that he planned to appoint "you two prima donnas" to the Council on the Environment and then sit back and watch the sparks fly. Instead, the two men held each other in great esteem, worked in perfect accord, and became great friends.[20]

Bemiss recalls that around this time he, Governor Holton, and Hanes also discussed the dam on the Rappahannock River at Fredericksburg, which blocked the passage of fish returning upstream from the ocean to breed. The dam was finally removed in 2005 after years of lobbying by the Friends of the Rappahannock and under the leadership of Senator John Warner. After the removal, the Rappahannock became the longest free-flowing river in Virginia, allowing shad and herring to travel freely up the Rappahannock and the Rapidan. In the 1960s, under the leadership of Mayor Josiah Rowe, the City of Fredericksburg purchased the stream frontage land from the Virginia Power Company, which had considered creating a reservoir upstream. In a deal negotiated and financed by The Nature Conservancy in 2006, the City gave the Virginia Outdoors Foundation, the Department of Game and Inland Fisheries, and The Nature Conservancy a perpetual conservation easement on sixty miles of upriver frontage on the Rappahannock and the Rapidan totaling 4,232 acres on land originally purchased from Virginia Power by the City. The Nature Conservancy is working to restore shad spawning habitat in the river today. George Freeman was special counsel to the City in the gift of that easement.[21]

Governor Holton's September 1970 executive order creating Virginia's Council on the Environment was the first instance in which the executive branch officially ordered an administrative action directly related to the environment. The council brought together state government agencies, ensuring coordination during the decision-making process. According to its first director, Gerald McCarthy, the council wanted to be sure that all pertinent state agencies were "running the same race at roughly the same speed and in the same direction."[22] Council participants included representatives from the Departments of Transportation, Agriculture, and Health; the State Corporation Commission; the attorney general's office; and the State Water Control Board, along with Hanes and Bemiss, who were appointed to represent the public. According to the *Richmond Times-Dispatch*, "Governor Holton underscored the importance he attached to the new advisory group by assuming the chairmanship himself during the critical early days of the Council. He then appointed Hanes as Chairman who served during the entire Holton Administration."[23] The council proceeded to hold hearings around the state to ascertain the public's views on the serious environmental issues of the day.

In its prime, the council issued annual reports on the condition of Virginia's environment, a constant reminder of efforts to clean up the air and water and to conserve open space. Holton's administration underscored its commitment when, in a plan to reorganize the executive branch, it pointedly established the Secretariat of Commerce and Natural Resources—the first time in Virginia history that the term "natural resources" was included in the title of a state body.

The council functioned as the Commonwealth's primary body for coordinating overall state policy at the state agency level through the Wilder administration, at which point it and the state's Water Control Board, Air Pollution Control Board, and Waste Management Board were transferred to separate units under a newly created Department of Environmental Quality. But this proved to be a step backward—the council, with its outside members representing the public, was no longer the coordinator of state environmental policy. It fell into disuse, and any enforcement declined rapidly during the administration of George Allen, when Allen's secretary of natural resources, Becky Norton Dunlop, declined to take advantage of it.[24]

When Governor Holton turned his attention to pollutant discharges in Virginia's waters, he made another important contribution. Under the 1972 federal Water Protection Act, commonly known as the Clean Water Act, Virginia's cities had to pay only 20 percent of the total cost of constructing new wastewater treatment facilities, with the balance coming from the state and federal government. Governor Holton secured an increase in the state income tax to fund Virginia's matching share of federal grants for enforcement of the Clean Water Act in Virginia. He tried to push through a cigarette tax, a formidable challenge in one of the nation's biggest tobacco-growing states. That effort failed, but in the process Philip Morris, which had opposed the tax, agreed to support the income tax increase.[25] Holton hoped that by the close of his term, with the completion of wastewater treatment facilities, "every river in Virginia would be 'swimmable,' except perhaps the Elizabeth River!"

Holton's commitment to clean rivers was exemplified by his appointment of Norman Cole to chair the new State Water Control Board. Widely recognized as a leading nuclear engineer, Cole had a passionate interest in cleaning up Virginia's polluted waterways, particularly the Potomac, which was both dangerous to swim in and unable to support a healthy fish or aquatic population. As chairman, Cole seized the reins of the fledgling state agency and transformed it into one of the most proactive and effective agencies of the Commonwealth.[26]

In the late 1960s, conservationists had been enraged over the proposal for a four-lane riverside parkway that would run along the south bank of the James River next to the falls of the James in the city of Richmond. A group led by Dr. R. B. Young, Louise Burke, and many others created the Richmond Scenic James Council to fight the proposal. Fortunately, at that time there was plenty of political momentum for protecting the environment following the adoption of the 1966 legislation of the Virginia Outdoors Plan, the enactment of the Scenic Rivers Act in 1970, and Article XI of the new state constitution of 1970. The Richmond Scenic James Council was thus able to persuade the Richmond City Council to abandon the proposed expressway in the riverbed and agree to designate the James River a Virginia scenic river. With the help of City Manager Alan Kiepper and others, George Freeman drafted the Historic Falls of the James Act, which was enacted by the General Assembly and signed into law by Governor Holton in 1972.[27]

During Holton's term from 1970 to 1974, Virginia acquired the lands for False Cape and Grayson Highlands state parks, an accomplishment in which Holton took great pride. No private or federal funds were spent on these acquisitions, and they marked the first time since 1936 that the "fiscally conservative" state had appropriated dedicated funds to acquire land for new state parks.[28]

Meanwhile, public demand for services was growing with Virginia's burgeoning population, and the state responded with massive building programs and highway projects, giving little or no thought to the environmental impacts of either. Recognizing this, Governor Holton called for yet another legislative study commission to review the environmental impact of all major state undertakings. The legislation that resulted from this review in 1973 mandated that all state agencies consider the possible negative consequences of new projects, and that they would be subject to review by the Council on the Environment.[29] Formerly, when it came to reviewing the environmental impact of any given project, the effects of state building and construction activities were the partial responsibility of several environmental agencies but the overall responsibility of none. Many of these agencies, and also universities, prisons, and the Highway Department, were accustomed to undertaking major construction projects without accounting for their possible deleterious effects on the environment. The new law placed responsibility on all agencies so that the risk of environmental side effects of state actions would be fully assessed in the planning stages.

The bill, fashioned after the federal NEPA, set a good example for the corporations and municipalities that it regulated and forced them to comply with clean air, water, and waste efforts. Not universally embraced at first, it formally acknowledged the state's responsibility for the environment and made Virginia one of the first states to require each agency to think through, document, and evaluate the environmental effects of its proposed actions.

By the mid-1970s there had been virtually no progress in cooperation among regional government sectors. A virulent annexation case had raged between Richmond and Chesterfield in the early years of the decade.[30] This and the construction of the Downtown Expressway, together with a federal appellate court reversal of a court order to consolidate the Richmond, Henrico, and Chesterfield school systems,[31] led to "white flight" from the core city. It also led ultimately to a moratorium on annexation throughout the state. This was a serious blow to cities that needed room to grow and sought to expand their tax bases and broaden efforts to create an integrated and unified metropolitan area. Neighboring jurisdictions failed in most instances to work together. Rather, they bickered, each seeking to protect its own turf, to the detriment of coordinated resource and land-use planning.

Richmond, encircled by growing suburban counties and landlocked by the 1965 Voting Rights Act, was forced to seek a remedy by raising local property taxes. This only exacerbated the problems, and Richmond citizens abandoned the city in even greater droves, seeking lower taxes and better schools in the surrounding counties. It also turned the clock back on Richmond's governance. The award of forty-one square miles of Chesterfield to Richmond in the annexation case was challenged under the Voting Rights Act as a dilution of Richmond's African

American vote. Lengthy litigation resulted in a settlement in which Richmond was redivided into electoral wards to ensure proportional racial representation on the city council; citywide representatives were eliminated. The resulting ward system endures to this day, although the fragmentation has been moderated somewhat by legislation permitting the election of Richmond's mayor by the voters at large and the election of former Virginia governor Douglas Wilder to that post.[32]

On the larger front, many of Virginia's rivers were still being polluted by municipal and industrial waste ("point-source pollution") and unfiltered runoff from paved shopping centers, fertilized farms and lawns, and clear-cut timbered areas ("nonpoint-source pollution"). For example, Allied Chemical Company had for years been dumping large quantities of kepone, a component of a deadly pesticide, into the James River.[33] In 1977, Judge Robert R. Merhige of the U.S. District Court for the Eastern District of Virginia assessed substantial fines and directed Allied Chemical to clean up the river. In addition, he suggested that the company provide $8 million to establish an endowment to benefit Virginia's environment. It was not a mandatory court order, but Allied Chemical complied with the innovative suggestion, and the initial $8 million in fines established the Virginia Environmental Endowment.

In the same year, Gerald McCarthy left the state's Council on the Environment to become the endowment's first (and only) director. Unprecedented in the federal system at the time, it was the only foundation funded under a federal court directive to focus exclusively on the environment. According to McCarthy, in the 1970s nearly all environmentalists perceived unregulated industry as the primary source of air and water pollution, and therefore as "the enemy."

To help clean up polluted waters and to buy fragile and threatened watersheds, the endowment made grants to environmental groups and businesses. It also awarded smaller grants for environmental education programs. The Virginia Center for Environmental Negotiation, dedicated to finding common ground between parties locked in legal battles over issues of land use and pollution, was one of the recipients of the endowment's largesse.[34]

The decade after *Virginia's Common Wealth* was released saw large-scale positive responses to Virginia's environmental problems. Environmental awareness reached a high point, as reflected in state and federal governmental and public support. Dedicated visionaries engaged environmental issues in practical ways, leading a willing populace onto the "right course." Governors Harrison, Godwin, and Holton articulated the importance of environmental protection to the well-being of the Commonwealth and gave concern for the environment a place at the table in developing state policy. Governor Holton in particular was a good friend to the environmental movement in Virginia, making the environment a top priority of state government. Without his leadership as governor, few of the accomplishments of 1970–75 would have occurred. Virginia's leading environmental advocates, FitzGerald Bemiss and George Freeman among them, joined citizens and scholars in leading private organizations that served as powerful environmental proponents in the public forum.

Governor Charles S. Robb, who served from 1982 to 1986, reinvigorated the focus on environmental protection initiated by his predecessors and provided an instrument that would sharpen that focus: the Governor's Commission on the Future of Virginia.[35] The commission was composed of former governors, business leaders, academics, and leaders from both political parties. Three familiar names—FitzGerald Bemiss, Gerald McCarthy, and John Hanes—were among its members.

In 1984 the commission issued a report called *Toward a New Dominion: Choices for Virginians,* which was intended to create support for improving Virginia's approach to protecting its vast natural resources. As chairman of the commission's Environmental and Natural Resources Committee, FitzGerald Bemiss played a leading role in writing the section entitled "Natural Resources: A Matter of Commitment." He articulated both the conditions and the challenges of Virginia's environment in the early 1980s. The thinking of caring environmentalists was effectively summarized in such sections as "Water Quality, Quantity, Distribution" and "Land Use."

In addition, during the same period, George Freeman was representing clients throughout the country in the application of the National Environmental Policy Act, the Clean Air Act, and the Clean Water Act, and was serving as a member of the congressional advisory committee on the Superfund Act.[36]

But the economic recession of the early 1980s, along with a new national philosophy, under Ronald Reagan, contending that "less government" was desirable, weakened public enthusiasm for anything other than economic growth, and jobs and development became the state's number-one priority. Support for the commission report petered out, and the apathy continued throughout the 1990s. Factors that threaten our environment—population growth, unplanned development, continuing and growing pollution, corporate and individual greed, the hostility of many builders, financiers, and real estate agents, the ongoing ideological advocacy of unfettered property rights, and the weakness of communal concern at all levels of state government—rolled on almost unchecked. Slowly but surely, these factors undermined environmental efforts across the Commonwealth. Sadly, they continue to thwart environmental protection efforts today.

Open-Space Land Conservation

I N THE FACE OF EXPLODING GROWTH and development after World War II, the Commonwealth did nothing to protect its open natural areas beyond designating a few state parks and some lands managed by the Department of Game and Inland Fisheries. The private sector made the first move when, in 1956, The Nature Conservancy formed a committee that ultimately helped establish Great Falls Park in the Potomac Gorge of western Fairfax County.[1]

It was not until 1965 that the state addressed its serious lack of land conservation programs by calling for the Open Space Land Act in *Virginia's Common Wealth*. The open space to be protected was meant to encompass unspoiled meadows, fields, healthy stands of trees, and dense forests that clean the air we breathe and protect our drinking water. The act became part of the legislative package of the Virginia Outdoors Plan, enacted in 1966. It authorized public bodies to "acquire or designate property for use as open-space land."

> To carry out the purposes of this chapter, any public body may (i) acquire by purchase, gift, devise bequest, grant or other wise title to, or any interests or rights of, not less than five years' duration in real property that will provide a means for the preservation of provisions of open-space land and (ii) designate any real property in which it has an interest of not less than

five years' duration to be retained and used for the preservation and provision of open-space land. Any such interest may also be perpetual.[2]

This law became the underpinning for Virginia's open-space easement program. Conservation easements protect prime farmland, watersheds, scenic views, historic landscapes, and wildlife habitats by permanently removing land from development. George Freeman, special counsel to the VORSC, had worked hard to construct the law, which was patterned after the "Little House" preservation program of the National Trust of Scotland. Scotland had used the easement concept to protect the small cottages, many of them "row houses" in small villages, it bought, rehabilitated, and then sold to private owners to live in. Freeman had argued with other Virginia lawyers who doubted that easements could be used for conservation purposes because they could not "run with the land" or be "perpetual," according to the common law of England that Virginia had inherited.[3] Fortunately, Freeman's wisdom prevailed.

Freeman and Gerry Bemiss knew that they needed to keep an eye out for any new federal or state laws or regulations that might interfere with Virginia's innovative conservation easement program. Their vigilance paid off soon after the 1966 Virginia laws were enacted, when the Internal Revenue Service proposed amendments to the Internal Revenue Code in 1968 that inadvertently would have eliminated a donor's ability to deduct the value of conservation easements when the donor lived on or used the property. This threatened the continuing viability of gifts of conservation easements from landowners, which were an important part of all federal and state conservation programs. Freeman did not learn of this until the day the House-Senate conference committee was meeting to reconcile conflicting sections of the tax code that had passed in both houses. He called Bemiss, and together they quickly drafted a letter from Bemiss to Senator Harry Byrd Jr., who was then a member of the Senate Finance Committee and one of the Senate conferees, suggesting language that would save the tax deduction for gifts of perpetual open-space easements. Freeman then drove the letter straight to Washington, where he found that the conference committee was already meeting in a closed-door session. Not one to give up easily, he persuaded Senator Byrd's chief aide to slip the letter to Byrd under the closed door of the meeting room. Someone picked up the letter and gave it to Byrd, and the recommended language ended up being incorporated into the conference report and ultimately into IRS regulations.[4] This last-minute rescue operation saved Virginia's conservation and historic preservation easement program, which went on to become one of the most effective in the nation. Countless examples of cooperation among the state, private conservation organizations, and generous citizens contributed to its success.

If the Open Space Land Act was the skeleton of the Commonwealth's conservation easement program, the Virginia Outdoors Foundation (VOF) was the muscle. The VOF and the Virginia Historic Landmarks Commission (VHLC) had been created under the 1966 Virginia Outdoors Plan legislative package. Whereas the Open Space Land Act generally authorized all state agencies and local governing bodies to accept easements, only the VOF and the VHLC were specifically entitled to receive easements on behalf of the state. This was accomplished through the provisions that created those two agencies: "The Virginia Outdoors Foundation is established to promote the preservation of open-space lands and to encourage private gifts of money, securities or other property to preserve the natural, scenic, historic, scientific, open-space and recreational areas of the Commonwealth."[5] Likewise, "the Board of Historic Resources may acquire by purchase or gift designated landmarks and sites or easements or interests therein."[6]

It was the owners of properties certified as historic Virginia landmarks who gave the first easements to the state. In 1969, Anne Maury White gave the VHLC the first easement, on the Old Mansion in Bowling Green, in Caroline County. During those early days the VOF was essentially dormant in promoting easements. As Tyson Van Auken, longtime VOF director, recalls, "With a paltry $125 in the bank, conservation was an insignificant sidebar." But the VOF soon came to life when, at Governor Holton's request, Clifford Schroeder became the first chair of its board. Schroeder had moved to Virginia from New

York, where he had been familiar with that state's private conservation efforts, and he was appalled by the growing degradation of Virginia's environment. Schroeder first turned to wealthy landowners in Northern Virginia who might be willing to place restrictive conservation easements on their rural estates. He called them "the low-hanging fruit," meaning that they were most likely to be receptive to donating easements to protect their open fields.[7]

After that, historic and open-space easements went reasonably smoothly, propelled by the timely concurrence of two major events relating to the Bull Run Mountains in Northern Virginia. The first was the designation in *Virginia's Common Wealth* of the Bull Run Mountains as a high-priority area for a state park.[8] The second was that Audrey and Stephen Currier, who owned a farm in Scott District of Fauquier County, adjacent to the mountains, had become alarmed by the threat of development of high-density subdivisions atop those mountains. The Curriers hired Theodore J. Wirth and Associates of Billings, Montana, to prepare a report, *A Proposal for the Establishment of the Bull Run Mountain Conservancy* (1970). The report proposed that two conservation zones be created: a mountain zone in Fauquier County and Prince William County running from Thoroughfare Gap northward to Aldie in Loudoun County, and a surrounding buffer zone in the three counties. The proposal stated:

> The justification for establishment of the Bull Run Conservancy is threefold:
> 1. A need for a conservancy in Northern Virginia regional area.
> 2. The preservation of a unique natural scenic area from being swallowed by suburban sprawl.
> 3. To provide, within the urban and northern regional area, a unique and substantially open space within easy reach of all the people.

The Curriers had initially approached The Nature Conservancy as a possible vehicle for assembling the land. But the arrangement fell through because the Conservancy doubted that it could maintain the secrecy necessary for such a large-scale land acquisition program. Rich-

White quartzite rocks
and stunted table-
mountain pines are
prominent features of
the cliffs at High Point,
the highest peak in the
Bull Run Mountains.
These white cliffs,
located several miles
north of Thoroughfare
Gap in Fauquier County,
Virginia, are visible to
drivers traveling from
the west. (© Gary P.
Fleming)

ard Pough, former president of The Nature Conservancy, then serving
on its board, was disappointed, but he soon found a solution by orga-
nizing an independent charitable foundation—the Natural Areas
Council—to do the job. Pough hired Bruce Dowling, who had been a
key member of The Nature Conservancy staff, to be the council's director. The council then engaged George Freeman to act as counsel in this
effort. Both Pough and Dowling knew Freeman from their earlier association in founding the Virginia chapter of the Conservancy. George
Freeman was a major participant in the monumental effort that followed over the next several decades to preserve Virginia's Bull Run
Mountains.

Audrey Currier made an initial contribution of $1.5 million to the Natural Areas Council, and Alice DuPont Mills directed the Chichester-DuPont Foundation to convey the 941-acre Roland property to the council. Freeman hired Donald Faulkner, a real estate agent known throughout Virginia as a specialist in hunt country–type rural real estate, as the lead agent to supervise acquisitions in the mountains. To maintain the secrecy of the overall acquisition effort, several of Freeman's law partners and other Richmond-area environmentalists served as nominal title holders for the properties purchased. Parcels totaling about twenty-nine hundred acres, consisting of the Roland estate and other lands held by the nominal title holders, were assembled by mid-1967.

Then a terrible event occurred: the Curriers disappeared in a tragic plane crash in the Caribbean. When their wills were probated, they contained no bequests to the Natural Areas Council, and the council had to resort to selling some of the properties held by its nominal title holders in order to close on purchase contracts then pending on other tracts in the mountains. But those sales took place only after perpetual open-space easements had been conveyed on them to the VOF.[9] After it became clear that no gifts were coming from the charitable trusts created by the Curriers' wills, the Natural Areas Council was forced to put the Bull Run project on hold. Thereafter, the council advanced funds from the America the Beautiful Fund to maintain properties the council had acquired.

In 1968 the Natural Areas Council started discussions with the Commonwealth on possible ways to complete the project. In 1972 the state tried to help complete part of it by creating a "natural areas" type of park, using Goshen Pass in Rockbridge County as a model, centered on the south end of the mountains at Thoroughfare Gap, with the entrance through the old mill site off U.S. Route I-66. But some local landowners in Scott District of Fauquier County opposed the project, and the state abandoned it.

In 1975, under an agreement reached at a meeting attended by the two Currier daughters, Andrea and Lavinia, Alice DuPont Mills, representatives of the Natural Areas Council and the VOF, and George Freeman, the council agreed to transfer its holdings in the Bull Run Mountains to the VOF. The actual transfer took place in 1979, and the VOF reimbursed the America the Beautiful Fund for monies it had advanced to the council for the maintenance of the properties. Since then the VOF has continued to acquire land with funds contributed by private individuals.

In 1994, Friends of Bull Run was founded as a nonprofit community organization and leased eight hundred acres of Bull Run Mountain land from the VOF to provide educational and recreational opportunities to the public. The 1996 Virginia Outdoors Plan and a 1997 study by Earth Design Associates recommended a master plan for preservation of the mountains and development of a trail traversing the ridges from Aldie Mill on the north to Thoroughfare Gap on the south. In 1998, the Virginia Department of Conservation and Recreation, through its Division of Natural Heritage, conducted a study of the mountains for their "(1) bio-geographic significance as a meeting ground for disjunct species from both the mountains and the Coastal Plain; (2) high quality and diversity of natural communities, including some that are uncommon or rare in the Piedmont; and (3) viability on an ecosystem scale due to a large, unfragmented forest cover and relatively pristine hydrology."[10] As a result, the department recommended natural area dedication as the most appropriate means of long-term, permanent conservation of VOF lands in this area. VOF trustees subsequently adopted a resolution accepting this recommendation and in the spring of 2002 formally dedicated it as such. The VOF continues to work with state resource agencies, conservation groups, citizens, and landowners in efforts to preserve the Bull Run Mountains.

Between 1966 and 1979 the Natural Areas Council also helped solicit open-space easement gifts from private landowners to the VOF on lands in Fauquier County's Scott District adjoining the Bull Run Mountains. This effort was picked up and substantially expanded later by the Piedmont Environmental Council (PEC), an organization that made a huge contribution to Virginia's open-space preservation.[11]

The Piedmont Environmental Council, founded in 1972 to "promote and protect the Piedmont's rural economy, natural resources, history and beauty," provides technical and legal expertise to citizens, local governments, and grassroots groups in a nine-county region of Virginia's northern Piedmont.[12] The organization was and remains to this day a strong advocate for land conservation and managed growth in Virginia. Since its inception it has worked with rural landowners to encourage them to donate conservation easements on their properties. The PEC still works closely with the VOF, and the majority of easements in the PEC's region are held by the VOF. More than 270,000 acres in the PEC's region were protected by conservation easements by the end of 2006, nearly 78,000 of them in Fauquier County.

The PEC has been directly involved with the Virginia Landmarks Register and the National Register listings of several rural historic districts, including the Southwest Mountains District and the Southern Albemarle District in Albemarle County,[13] the Madison Barbour District in Orange County, and the Crooked Run Valley District in Fauquier County.[14] In the nearly twenty years since the Southwest Mountains and Madison Barbour districts in Albemarle and Orange counties were approved, approximately 30 percent of the land in each district has been protected by landowners who have voluntarily donated conservation easements. These two contiguous historic districts are among the largest districts in the Commonwealth, each encompassing nearly thirty thousand acres. In 2002, with PEC assistance, Fauquier County conducted a historic survey that identified twenty-one villages and four rural areas eligible for the Virginia Landmarks Register and National Register of Historic Places. Eleven of these villages and two rural historic districts have been listed on the registers since 2003.

Starting in 2006 the PEC took the initiative to oppose Dominion Power in its effort to run a forty-mile-long, 500,000-volt transmission line through seven counties in Virginia's historic northern Piedmont.[15] The proposed towers would stand fifteen stories tall and cut a two-hundred-foot-wide scar across a landscape that today looks much as it did when George Washington surveyed the region more than two hundred years ago, thanks largely to citizen and governmental initiatives. The line would slash through historic sites and districts, magnificent view sheds, publicly held open space, and a high concentration of conservation easements. At risk from the actual transmission line or its significant negative visual impact are seven major Civil War battle-fields, eleven historic districts listed on the Virginia and National registers and seven proposed historic districts; nineteen historic sites on the Virginia and National registers; forty-eight thousand acres of conservation easements; eighty-three miles of officially designated scenic byways; ten miles of scenic rivers; and thirteen miles of the Appalachian Trail.

The venerable and hard-working Nature Conservancy continued to play a huge role in Virginia's open-space preservation after the 1960s.[16] The approach of the Conservancy is nonconfrontational, science based, and solution oriented. As John Sawhill, Conservancy president from 1989 to 2000, often put it, "We get results you can walk around on."

After its formation in 1960, the Virginia chapter of The Nature Conservancy remained an all-volunteer organization until it hired its first staff in 1980. During the 1960s and 1970s the Virginia chapter worked with the Conservancy's national headquarters to protect several outstanding natural areas. Wildcat Mountain became the Conservancy's first Virginia preserve in 1961, when it was donated by the Arundel family. Much more recently, the Arundel family donated an additional 258 acres, and George and Rab Thompson donated a 1,192-acre conservation easement to increase the size of Wildcat Mountain Preserve. Other acquisitions in the 1960s included thirteen hundred acres on Mt. Rogers, Virginia's highest peak (on behalf of the U.S. Forest Service); Mason Neck National Wildlife Refuge; Fraser Preserve, on the Potomac River in Fairfax County; "Fernbrook," in Albemarle County; the Alexander Berger tract outside Fredericksburg; and ninety-seven acres on Botetourt County's Tinker Mountain for the Appalachian Trail.

In the 1970s, the Conservancy moved to science-based strategic actions to protect the Commonwealth's best natural areas. Bob Jenkins, the Conservancy's first director of science, pioneered a database-driven biological inventory system that came to be known as the Natural Heritage Program, which the Conservancy has now established in all fifty states in cooperation with state governments. States use the biological

Old stone walls meander through the Wildcat Mountain Natural Area, The Nature Conservancy's first preserve in Virginia, located near Warrenton in Fauquier County. (Photo by Mary Porter, courtesy of The Nature Conservancy)

inventory for environmental review and to set priorities for land acquisition. Fulfilling another 1965 recommendation of *Virginia's Common Wealth,* the Virginia Natural Heritage Program was established in the Department of Conservation and Historic Resources in 1989, during the Baliles administration, Michael Lipford serving as its director. In 1994 it was named the outstanding Natural Heritage Program in the Western Hemisphere.

One of The Nature Conservancy's most ambitious undertakings was preserving the barrier islands along Virginia's Eastern Shore. In 1965, *Virginia's Common Wealth* had targeted Parramore Island as a potential state park. Parramore is the largest of the offshore islands, situated midway between the federally owned Assateague-Chincoteague National Seaside Park and the state's Mockhorn Island Wildlife Management Area. In the late 1960s, Eastern Shore lawyer and conservationist Benjamin Mears learned that a group of Norfolk-area businessmen was interested in buying another of the islands, Little Cobb.[17] Mears called George Freeman to see if he could persuade The Nature Conservancy to purchase Little Cobb or at least provide the funds to purchase an option, which the owner was willing to sell. When the Conservancy declined, Freeman approached Bruce Dowling of the Natural Areas Council, with whom he was working on the Bull Run conservancy project. The Natural Areas Council came through with the option money in the form of a grant from the America the Beautiful Fund, and the option agreement was signed. Later, however, when it appeared that the funds for its exercise could not be obtained from private or public sources, Freeman negotiated a gentlemen's understanding with the Norfolk businessmen. He would stand aside and allow them to purchase Little Cobb, but with the understanding that they would not develop it so long as there was a reasonable chance that a comprehensive offshore islands protection effort could be launched successfully.

That occurred in 1970, when The Nature Conservancy purchased its first barrier island through a grant from the Mary Flagler Charitable Trust. The acquisition of Metompkin Island was a welcome if belated triumph for the members of the Virginia Outdoor Recreation Study Commission.[18] Under the initial leadership of Patrick Noonan, president of the Conservancy from 1973 to 1984, and guided by the steady hand of Gregory Low through the 1980s and 1990s, the Conservancy launched the Virginia Coast Reserve Project, which has protected fourteen barrier islands and several seaside and bayside farms, totaling some fifty thousand acres. The Virginia Environmental Endowment provided funds in 1977 to enable the Conservancy to locate a staff and acquire a headquarters for its Eastern Shore operations, and subsequently to launch the Virginia Coast Reserve Program in Nassawaddox. Most of the seaside farms acquired by the Conservancy have been resold to private landowners with conservation easements to protect them. The Conservancy also helped establish the Eastern Shore National Wildlife Refuge, the first property one encounters when emerging from the Chesapeake Bay Bridge Tunnel, adding significant acreage in 2006 under the leadership of Senator Warner. The Conservancy worked with the state to add Magothy Natural Area Preserve in 2006. The Virginia Coast Reserve remains today as the last protected undeveloped barrier island system on the eastern seaboard.

Hog Island Coast Reserve, located along the Atlantic coast of the Eastern Shore, offers breathtaking views and unspoiled beauty. (Photo by Hal Brindley, courtesy of The Nature Conservancy)

The Nature Conservancy achieved another success in 1973, when Patrick Noonan persuaded Union Camp Corporation to donate fifty thousand acres of corporate timberland in Virginia's Great Dismal Swamp. This was the first time a private business had given land for conservation purposes in Virginia and was one of the first corporate gifts to a conservation charity in the nation. Later gifts and acquisitions from Union Camp brought the total acreage in the Great Dismal Swamp National Wildlife Refuge to 110,000 acres, making it one of the largest contiguous blocks of protected forest land on the eastern seaboard.[19]

In the mid-1980s, Virginia Beach was one of the fastest-growing localities in the nation. During this period the Conservancy and the Department of Conservation together protected nearly ten thousand acres of significant wetlands along North Landing River. But Virginia Beach was struggling to prevent development from overtaking productive farmlands adjacent to those wetlands in the city's southern reaches. Working with farmers, the city council, other government officials, and concerned citizens, the Conservancy proposed the first purchase of development rights (PDR) program in the Commonwealth. In 1995, the Virginia Beach City Council adopted an ordinance creating the Agricultural Reserve Program, which targeted twenty thousand acres of farmland for protection through easement purchases. To date, the program has successfully protected more than seventy-five hundred acres.

The Conservancy then protected more than six thousand acres along the Northwest River in the neighboring city of Chesapeake, to maintain a wildlife corridor from the Dismal Swamp to the Currituck Sound. One of the state's newest wildlife management areas was established along the river in 2005, when the Conservancy worked with International Paper and the Department of Game and Inland Fisheries to protect the four-thousand-acre Cavalier tract.

In 1985, at the opposite end of the state, the Conservancy established its Clinch Valley Program, which sought to protect the last free-flowing section of the Tennessee River system. Threatened by large-scale logging on the steep mountains surrounding the river, the Conservancy began in 1984 with acquisition of Pendleton Island in the Clinch River, the most biologically diverse river in the United States. When the threat of logging on the surrounding mountains increased, the Conservancy started the Conservation Forestry Program in the late 1990s. Since 2002 the owners of Stuart Land and Cattle Company, one of America's oldest cattle ranches, have enrolled about ten thousand acres of its land in this program. These historic lands once raised horses for one of the family's renowned ancestors, General J. E. B. Stuart, and the Confederate cavalry he commanded. Under the forest management easement program designed with legal assistance from the Virginia chapter's board chairman, Thurston Moore, Conservancy staff members conduct sustainable logging operations that generate revenue for annual payments to landowners. This working forest agreement is mutually beneficial to the water quality of the river and the landowner, who retains ownership of the land and is guaranteed an annual income in perpetuity. The ranch borders the state's 25,477-acre Clinch Mountain Wildlife Management Area, most of which was for-

Rich Mountain Farm straddles Russell and Washington counties in Southwest Virginia's Clinch River Valley. The Stuart Land & Cattle Company, which owns the oldest continuously operated ranch in the United States, enrolled more than 5,700 acres of Rich Mountain Farm in The Nature Conservancy's Conservation Forestry Program in 2002. (Photo by Mundy Hackett, courtesy of The Nature Conservancy)

merly owned by the Stuarts. The Conservancy recently acquired Brumley Mountain, another adjacent property of five thousand acres, from a developer who had planned to subdivide the property. In 2007 it was transferred to the Commonwealth as Southwest Virginia's first state forest.

The Conservancy has also been active in protecting land along the tributaries of the Chesapeake Bay. In 1987, Dr. Mitchell Byrd of the College of William and Mary approached the Conservancy about protecting the eastern seaboard's largest summer roosting site for bald eagles. In 1989 the group purchased thirty-five hundred acres of land along the James River in Prince George County, which later became the James River National Wildlife Refuge.

In 1994 the Conservancy acquired Cumberland Marsh Preserve, eleven hundred acres on the Pamunkey River in New Kent County, and a conservation easement on Upper Brandon Plantation. The easement—

negotiated with the James River Paper Company with the assistance of Conservancy chapter board member Dick Erickson and held jointly with the American Farmland Trust—protects one of the oldest continuously cultivated farms in Virginia. The Conservancy, along with the Chesapeake Bay Foundation, also was active in creating the Rappahannock River Valley National Wildlife Refuge. In 1999, with the assistance of Senator John Warner, the Conservancy acquired Toby's Point in Richmond County from Alan Voorhees for the refuge. Two new state forests were protected by the Conservancy in cooperation with Jim Garner, formerly a member of the Conservancy's board and the state forester, twenty-two hundred acres on the Mattaponi River, purchased by the Conservancy in 2000, and eighteen hundred acres along Dragon Run, purchased in 2003.

In recent years the Conservancy has turned its attention to an alarming trend—the sale of vast tracts of forest that corporations have assembled and held for more than a century. In 2002 the Conservancy purchased from Virginia Hot Springs, Inc., nearly ten thousand acres on and around Warm Springs Mountain adjacent to the Homestead resort in Bath County. In its largest single purchase in Virginia, the Conservancy protected the most threatened and biologically significant private tract of forest in the Alleghenies of western Virginia. Warm Springs Mountain Preserve shares a thirteen-mile border with George Washington National Forest and holds together more than 175,000 acres of public land. Today the Conservancy manages this property as a demonstration site for proper forest management and restoration.

In 2005, International Paper announced the sale of its landholdings in the United States—nearly 1.2 million acres. The lands to be sold in Virginia totaled 150,000 acres. The Conservancy negotiated a huge private land conservation sale in 2006, acquiring 218,000 acres across ten states. The historic transaction protected more than twenty thousand acres in Virginia, including a five-thousand-acre tract called Big Woods that borders the twenty-seven-hundred-acre Piney Grove Preserve in Sussex County. The Conservancy is restoring habitat at this preserve for Virginia's rarest bird, the red-cockaded woodpecker, which inhabits only fire-dependent, old-growth pine forests. Private investors hold the remaining fifteen thousand acres along the Nottoway, Meherrin, and Blackwater rivers. The Conservancy retains the right of first negotiation on these river properties, some of which feature centuries-old bald cypress trees.

As monumental as these acquisitions are, they represent only the first step in efforts to protect the last remaining unbroken forests in eastern Virginia. John Hancock Forest Investments acquired most of the Chesapeake Corporation's land and will soon sell more than twenty thousand acres along Dragon Run in the Middle Peninsula, mostly in the county of King and Queen. Mead/Westvaco recently announced plans to sell its landholdings in five states, including 165,000 acres in Virginia's southern Piedmont. Protecting these forests intact will require creative strategies, partnerships, and money.

Today the Conservancy is poised to work at an even greater scale. The global organization has set a goal to protect 10 percent of all major habitat types on earth by 2015. As part of that effort, the Virginia chapter is working with neighboring states on four large-scale global priorities close to home: the central Appalachian forests and rivers, the Chesapeake Bay and its tributaries, the Albemarle-Pamlico Sound and its tributaries, and the Mid-Atlantic Seascape, the last a pioneering marine conservation effort off Virginia's coast. None of this happens through the work of the Conservancy alone, but rather through generous donations of private individuals, landowners, and foundations, as well as partnerships with private organizations, land trusts, and public agencies. Land conservation in Virginia has often been spurred by the passion of a single individual or a small group of dedicated individuals, like those who helped pioneer this movement in Mrs. Bocock's living room in 1960.

Another hero in the fight to preserve open space in Virginia is the Civil War Preservation Trust (CWPT), a nonprofit national organization that paid $12 million for a 208-acre farm in Spotsylvania County known as the Slaughter Pen Farm and associated with the 1862 battle of Fredericksburg. The trust then donated an easement on the parcel to the Virginia Historic Landmarks Board, successor to the Virginia Historic Landmarks Commission. Other battlefield easements donated

Brandy Station Battlefield, site of the "most hotly contested cavalry engagement of the Civil War," according to the *Civil War Battlefield Guide* (published by the Conservation Fund in 1990), is located in rural Culpeper County, Virginia. (Virginia Department of Historic Resources)

to the Board of Historic Resources by the CWPT include nearly 30 acres at the Brandy Station battlefield in Culpeper County, 345 acres at Petersburg's "breakthrough battlefield," and 134 acres at Chancellorsville in Spotsylvania County. The CWPT anticipates that this land will become part of the National Park Service's Fredericksburg-Spotsylvania National Battlefield Park.[20] The Chancellorsville Park leapfrogs westward along state Route 3, from Fredericksburg to the Wilderness battlefield.[21]

The Wildlife Foundation of Virginia, another Virginia conservation organization, purchased a 550-acre tract in the Blue Ridge Mountains just west of Graves Mill in Madison County, with plans to transfer the parcel to the Virginia Department of Game and Inland Fisheries (VDGIF) for public hiking and fishing. The mission of the VDGIF is "to manage Virginia's wildlife and inland fish to maintain optimum populations of all species to serve the needs of the Commonwealth; to provide opportunity for all to enjoy wildlife, inland fish, boating and related outdoor recreation; to promote safety for persons and property in connection with boating, hunting and fishing."[22] Although open land conservation is not strictly part of the agency's mission, Game and Inland Fisheries controls large undeveloped acreage in Virginia to provide habitat for biological resources and to offer hiking and fishing opportunities for the public.

Since 1988 a number of new private land trust and conservation organizations have been founded in Virginia.[23] They are a measure of the growing support for land conservation and the public's search for ways, at the local and regional levels, to help save fast-disappearing open space. More than forty organizations in Virginia have accepted donations or purchased conservation easements, while conducting programs to encourage good stewardship of natural resources.

Let us turn from the enormous private-sector effort for open-space protection since 1966 and turn to the history of Virginia's governmental actions that have helped or harmed the cause over the years since the publication of *Virginia's Common Wealth*. In 1977, Virginia's state legislature passed a law allowing landowners to place farmland or forested property in a "district," which then prohibited them from using that land for any use other than agriculture or timbering. In return, landowners received a reduction in their local real estate taxes. If landowners later removed their land from the agricultural or forestry district, they had to pay additional real estate tax to make up for the local government's "losses" in property tax revenues in back years. If the property had been subject to an open-space easement during those years, however, no refund would be due because under Virginia law the land subject to the easement could not have been assessed at a rate any higher than the county's land-use valuation in effect in the district during that time.

These taxation agreements were binding for five years and could be renewed. Within the designated districts, the state agencies responsible for soil and water conservation worked closely with farmers to develop "best management" plans to ensure that the farmland was used in a way that did the least damage to the environment.[24] Land-use taxation offered a lesser alternative than a perpetual open-space easement for farmers who were reluctant to tie up their land permanently.

But from a public land-use perspective, land-use taxation was less than ideal because, unlike an open-space or conservation easement, agricultural and forestry districts did not ensure permanent open-space protection.

In 1984, Governor Charles Robb authorized a Commission on Virginia's Future, which produced a report called *Toward a New Dominion: Choices for Virginians*. The commission's Environmental and Natural Resources Task Force prepared a section of the report, written by FitzGerald Bemiss, John Hanes, and Gerald McCarthy, that moved beyond previous state efforts for open-space land conservation. As in 1970–71, when the Council on the Environment held public hearings, public hearings were once again held around the state, which evoked strong statements calling for Virginia to pay greater attention to its environment. Eighty percent of survey respondents expressed support for environmental initiatives such as conserving open land and cleaning up waterways. Particularly telling was the report's final recommendation that the General Assembly revisit the findings and recommendations of the Virginia Outdoors Plan of 1966 and revise the plan to address worsening developments since enactment of its legislation package.[25]

The report came at a time when support for the environment at the national level was waning. The Reagan administration's policy was that government should do less for conservation and preservation and leave greater responsibility for land-use decisions to the private sector and the marketplace. Reagan's secretary of the interior, James Watt, was openly hostile to the environment, going so far as to advocate the elimination of the Land and Water Conservation Fund, the primary source of federal funding for state conservation efforts and a resource for land purchases for new state parks in Virginia. The National Wildlife Federation called for Watts's removal from office on the grounds that he assigned a far higher priority to development and exploitation than to conservation of the nation's natural resources.[26]

Governor Robb's term ended before the passionate plea in the Commission on Virginia's Future report could be answered. Fortunately his successor, Gerald Baliles, shared Robb's vision. With Governor Baliles's support, the Open Space Land Act was updated in 1988, confirming that any public body could acquire land by purchase, gift, or bequest, and directing that any covered acquisition or designation had to conform to the official comprehensive plan for the area in which it was located.

In addition, the Virginia Conservation Easement Act was passed in 1988. This act made clear that nonprofit groups like The Nature Conservancy need not purchase land in order to protect it but could hold conservation easements just as the VOF and the VHLC had been specifically authorized to do since 1966.[27] But the new law imposed conditions on charitable organizations or land trusts that wanted to accept such easements after the act's effective date. Years later, in 2005, the Virginia Supreme Court confirmed the validity of the Virginia Conservation Easement Act.[28]

Another progressive development in the 1980s was a partnership between the state and the private sector to identify and help protect fragile and significant biological and botanical species in "natural areas." Funds from the Virginia Environmental Endowment and Virginia Power had helped the state establish a program to gather data on endangered species in Virginia. In 1986 the newly named Natural Heritage Program became an official state program housed in the Department of Conservation. Two years later the state assumed full responsibility for its funding. The Nature Conservancy also worked with the department in an effort called "Partners in Conservation" and contributed $500,000 to acquire nine new natural areas with habitats for rare and endangered plants and animals and significant natural communities, most allowing public access.[29]

After 1988 progress toward protection of the environment began to wane. The post-Baliles years saw two major trends in the state government's approach to preserving open space. On the negative side, the state's commitment to funding its conservation and preservation agencies diminished, in part because of an economic downturn. By then Virginia was one of the few states along the eastern seaboard without a dedicated fund for land conservation, even as the neighboring states of Maryland and North Carolina were dedicating funds for that purpose. Also, even though Governor Baliles had earmarked funds from Virginia's lottery for conservation purposes, in the face of economic slowdown the General Assembly redirected the lottery money to the state's general fund, where it was used to balance the budget and pay for higher priorities. In addition, the 1992 general obligation bond funds were limited to the acquisition of parks and natural areas and could not be used for operation and maintenance. The Warner administration guided through the legislature another general obligation bond for parks and natural areas in 2002, but more permanent funding for land conservation had to wait. State officials had other priorities in the first years of the new century.

On the positive side, Virginia's perpetual open-space easement program became the most successful in the nation, thanks largely to the generosity of Virginia landowners. The boom in easement gifts was stimulated in part by a bill promoted by The Nature Conservancy and passed in 1999. The enactment of the Virginia Land Conservation Incentives Act of 1999 gave Virginia taxpayers who donated a conservation easement in 2000 and subsequent years a tax credit against state income tax liabilities of 50 percent of the value of the easement. The amount of the credit in any one year could not exceed $100,000, but any unused credit could be carried forward for an additional five years. In 2002 the General Assembly amended the law to permit taxpayers to transfer portions of credits for easements donated after January 1, 2002.

Ever since the publication of *Virginia's Common Wealth* in 1965, Virginia landowners have generously given open-space easements on their lands and historic landmarks. Forty-two years later, in September 2007, the Virginia Outdoors Foundation held perpetual open-space easements on a total of 412,785 acres in the state. Some of those easements were held jointly with the Board of Historic Resources, which also separately held easements on more than four hundred of the Commonwealth's certified historic landmarks and an additional 15,790 acres. Local governments hold easements totaling 9,759 acres. And ten of the twenty-six qualified 501(c)(3) charitable organizations held perpetual open-space easements on a total of 63,151 acres under Virginia's

1988 Conservation Easements Act. Finally, in September 2007 the federal government held easements on 5,766 acres in Virginia for historic and open-space preservation. The grand total of Virginia's open space protected by perpetual easements held by both public and private entities thus reached a total of 507,251 acres.[30]

Historic Preservation

W HEN THE MEMBERS of the Virginia Outdoor Recreation Study Commission took on the study of the environment in 1965, they realized that the environment to be protected included not just water, air, open space, and forests, but also the state's "vast historic treasure"—its historic, architectural, and archaeological sites of state-wide or national significance. *Virginia's Common Wealth* called for the creation of a new state agency, the Virginia Historic Landmarks Commission (VHLC) to address Virginia's built environment.[1] In the context of the White House "Beauty for America" Conference and the publication of *With Heritage So Rich,* a 1966 report of a special committee on historic preservation under the auspices of the U.S. Conference of Mayors, historic preservationists joined the environmental movement.[2] In the same year Congress passed the National Historic Preservation Act, the enabling legislation for the federal government's preservation programs.

Historic preservation has a long history in Virginia, thanks largely to the efforts of generations of women's groups that strove to save the homes of Virginia's heroes. The Mount Vernon Ladies' Association of the Union was organized in the mid-nineteenth century. The founding of the Association for the Preservation of Virginia Antiquities (APVA) in 1888 was motivated by the collapse of Powhatan's Chimney in Gloucester County; Norfolk's Mary Jeffrey Galt gathered some friends from Richmond and Williamsburg and modeled the new organization after the Mount Vernon Ladies' Association.[3] In the early 1890s the Confederate Memorial Ladies' Association saved the White House of the Confederacy in Richmond. In the 1920s a group in Fredericksburg formed a chapter of the Daughters of the American Revolution to save Kenmore, the home of George Washington's sister Betty and her husband, Fielding Lewis.

The William Byrd Branch of the APVA in Richmond, inspired by local preservationists Mary Wingfield Scott and Elizabeth Scott Bocock, spearheaded efforts to found the Historic Richmond Foundation in 1957. This organization, one of the nation's oldest and most effective local preservation groups, was responsible for saving much of the nineteenth-century neighborhood known as Church Hill and other historic houses in what is left of historic downtown Richmond.

Meanwhile, the APVA acquired and preserved historic properties all over Virginia, focusing on Virginia's colonial and antebellum periods. The Jamestown Island sites of the colonial church ruins, a graveyard, a colonial fort, and some Civil War earthworks were acquired by donation from Edward E. Barney in 1893.[4]

In 1926 the Reverend W. A. R. Goodwin, rector of Bruton Parish Church in Williamsburg, persuaded wealthy philanthropist John D. Rockefeller Jr. to fund the restoration or reconstruction of historic buildings in that colonial capital. Thus was born Colonial Williamsburg, serving as a classroom for eighteenth-century history and spurring efforts to save or restore other historic buildings across the Commonwealth and the nation.[5]

In 1966, with the creation of the Virginia Historic Landmarks Commission, Virginia's historic preservation program "took on a life of its own," according to Dr. Junius R. Fishburne Jr., historian and former VHLC director.[6] The state now defined historic properties as part of Virginia's environmental treasure. The mandate of the fledgling agency was to identify, survey, and evaluate significant buildings, sites, and districts associated with the Commonwealth's history. The law authorizing the VHLC called for the publication of a Virginia Landmarks Register, an expandable official list of resources that reflected Virginia's history. Beyond merely compiling a significant honor roll, the law directed the VHLC to provide tangible and technical help to owners of landmarks and to local governments. The Landmarks Register was an educational tool as well, informing the public that historic buildings had intrinsic value. Later in 1966, federal legislation created the National Register of Historic Places, a comparable national registry that would guide all levels of government as they coped with growth and development. Again, Virginia led the way.

The VHLC began its work in 1967 with a modest budget of $145,000. Stressing the importance of the new agency, legislators directed that representatives from the most respected statewide institutions serve on the new commission. Experts in history, historical architecture, landscape architecture, and archaeology were all included. The first chairman, Dr. Edward P. Alexander, was director of education and interpretation for Colonial Williamsburg.[7] John Melville Jennings, VHLC's vice chair, was director of the Virginia Historical Society. Randolph Church, the state librarian, Em Bowles Locker Alsop of the APVA, and Frederick Doveton Nichols, professor at the University of Virginia School of Architecture, represented their respective constituencies. Other members of the first VHLC were Stanley W. Abbott, landscape architect from Williamsburg; Marvin M. Sutherland, director of the Department of Conservation; Dr. Frederick Herman of Norfolk, representing the American Institute of Architects; and William R. Seward of Petersburg.

The VHLC selected James W. Moody, a preservation professional from Tennessee, as its first director. Under the new federal law authorizing the National Register of Historic Places, the VHLC director also served as the state historic preservation officer for Virginia, which meant that Moody and his staff were responsible for running the federal program in Virginia. Virginia Landmarks Register criteria and all other historic preservation activity followed federal guidelines. Reviewing federal projects for their effect on historic properties fell to the VHLC, and in return Virginia received federal funds to help defray the costs of its preservation program.

The VHLC developed property information files that became the heart of its work. The staff gathered historical, architectural, and geographical data from surveys conducted in the 1950s by the Historic American Buildings Survey Inventory, supplemented by historical information gathered in the 1930s by scholars working for the Works Progress Administration. VHLC staff visited many properties recorded in the Historic American Building Survey Inventory, photographing the buildings and marking them on U.S. Geological Survey maps. By July 1968, when the first VHLC report was submitted to the governor, the staff had visited historic buildings in every county in the state. Today the VHLC's successor agency, the Department of Historic Resources, maintains files on more than 183,200 buildings and archaeological sites across the state. These materials—maps, photographs, and historical data—collected in the course of surveying historic properties, have enabled the nomination of hundreds of buildings, sites, and structures for listing on the Virginia and National registers.[8]

The 1966 Virginia Outdoors Plan legislation had authorized both the VHLC and the Virginia Outdoors Foundation to hold perpetual easements on historic properties listed on the Virginia Landmarks Register. The preservation easement program proved to be a more effective and less costly tool for saving historic homes and other buildings than government purchase or public ownership. George Freeman, the originator of the easement legislation, convinced key state legislators that Virginia should encourage the preservation of privately owned historic landmarks by obtaining permanent legal protection of them while keeping them in private ownership and on the tax rolls. He believed that the best caretakers of historic properties, particularly residential ones, were their owners.[9]

The legislation had been crafted so that easements carried appreciable financial benefits for the donors as well as the preservation benefit to the Commonwealth. In exchange for relinquishing the right to develop their properties or tear down their houses, donors could count on several tax breaks. Because the perpetual easement restrictions generally reduced the fair market value of a property, the difference in

Located in rural Halifax County, Virginia, Berry Hill, a National Historic Landmark described as "a premier monument of the American Greek Revival," is listed on both the National and Virginia landmarks registers. (Virginia Department of Historic Resources)

value before and after application of an easement, as determined by a real estate appraiser, could be taken as a charitable tax deduction on both federal and state income taxes.

In addition to tax benefits, the easements allowed for adaptive reuse of a property that was in line with the preservation values being protected, under the rationale that new functions often instill new life in old buildings. For example, the Branch House, on Richmond's Monument Avenue, described by the VHLC's then senior architectural historian, Calder Loth, as "one of the country's finest examples of the Tudor-Jacobean style," now houses the headquarters of the Center for Virginia Architecture. And the stately Greek Revival mansion at Berry Hill in Halifax County, having gone from residence to training center to resort, is now slated to become part of a college campus.

The first easement forms for the Virginia Historic Landmarks Commission and the Virginia Outdoors Foundation were drafted in simple, straightforward language that could be understood by laymen as well as lawyers. George Freeman made speeches on the garden club circuit throughout Virginia to explain the easements and their tax benefits to potential donors. Today the easements are much more complex, largely because of ever-growing IRS regulations.

When, in 1969, Governor Mills Godwin accepted the easement for the 128-acre property of Old Mansion in Caroline County, which contained an important colonial manor house, it was to preserve the land as well as the house, which was built in 1670. The family of the donor, Anne Maury White, had owned Old Mansion for many generations and wanted to save the plantation for future generations as well. When the Virginia Department of Transportation wanted to acquire a sizable portion of the Old Mansion property to build a highway bypass around Bowling Green because that was the cheapest alternative route, it asked the VHLC board to release the preservation easement on the land. The board held a public hearing at the Transportation Department's request and concluded that it could not do so under the stringent criteria set forth in the statute.[10] The highway segment was built elsewhere. George Freeman represented the landowners in these proceedings. Fortunately, the 1966 Open Space Land Act had addressed this potential threat to open-space preservation—condemnation by state or local governments for other public purposes. At that time the threat appeared most likely to come from proposed new roads and highways. In hindsight we can see that perpetual open-space easements held by "public bodies" under that act also offer protection against efforts to destroy open space and historic structures by condemnation for urban renewal, a major problem today in some other states.[11]

The VHLC encountered its first major controversy involving state-owned property in the early 1970s, when the state bought two hundred acres in rural Louisa County for a new prison facility. This provoked an outcry of opposition to what was viewed as a threat to the historic agricultural area known as Green Springs. The Green Springs area had been farmed since the eighteenth century and retained much of its rural landscape and many historic farmhouses. Governor Holton, faced with local opposition led by landowner, attorney, and ardent preserva-

The Commonwealth's first preservation easement ensures perpetual protection of Old Mansion, an exceptionally significant landmark colonial mansion that stands adjacent to the county seat of Bowling Green in Caroline County, Virginia. (Virginia Department of Historic Resources)

tionist Rae Ely, offered to withdraw the state's proposal to build a prison if "the area could be preserved."[12]

In 1973 the VHLC responded to Governor Holton's requirement by listing the Green Springs Historic District on the Virginia Landmarks Register and nominating it for the National Register of Historic Places. Stanley Abbott, a VHLC member, respected landscape architect, and advocate for special rural landscapes in Virginia, strongly supported the registration of Green Springs as a historic landmark.[13] To prevent their holdings from being taken by the state for a new prison, or from being devalued by the presence of a prison in their neighborhood, many landowners in the new district donated protective easements to Historic Green Springs, Inc., a Virginia nonprofit corporation. A measure of Green Springs's significance was its recognition in 1974 as a

National Historic Landmark, the highest honor accorded by the federal government.

The Virginia Supreme Court explained what it meant to be listed on the Virginia Landmarks Register in a 1976 case related to the Green Springs Historic District.[14] The court called official landmark recognition a "hortatory act." That is, recognition as a Virginia landmark was defined as "an act of encouragement"—and not an edict—to the owner to care for and preserve the historic property.[15] More specifically, being listed on the Virginia Landmarks Register did not prevent property owners from using their landmark in any way they wished.[16] Fortunately, pressure from other landowners ultimately forced the mining company that owned the property involved in that case to withdraw its mining plans.

Historic Green Springs, Inc., later transferred its easements to the U.S. government, and they are now managed by the National Park Ser-

Green Springs National Historic District, described on the Virginia Landmarks Register as an "area long known for its exceptional fertility, prosperity, and beauty," was first settled in the early eighteenth century. It derives its name from a mineral spring located in the 14,000-acre bowl, "a geological formation that defines the district" in Louisa County, Virginia. (Virginia Department of Historic Resources)

vice. Recently a new landowner in the historic district tried to get the courts to declare that a preservation easement on his property given by a previous owner in 1973 to Historic Green Springs was invalid. Fortunately, the Virginia Supreme Court rejected his arguments.[17]

The VHLC's role in seeking recognition for the exceptional landscape of Green Springs was quite a debut for a small state agency that was not accustomed to newspaper headlines. The VHLC worked hard in subsequent years to convince a skeptical public that formally recognizing buildings as "historic" did not usually restrict private property rights. But being listed on the National Register of Historic Places or being eligible for such designation did mean an environmental review at the federal level and ensured that all feasible alternatives had to be explored before any action detrimental to the historic resource could take place.

VHLC staff documented archaeological sites across the Commonwealth, inspired by VHLC member and archaeologist Ivor Noël Hume, which led to official recognition for many of the sites.[18] One significant prehistoric site was Cactus Hill in Sussex County, where human occupation dated back nearly fifteen thousand years. Using funds donated by Anheuser-Busch, VHLC staff conducted an in-depth archaeological survey of the seventeenth- and eighteenth-century Kingsmill Plantation near Williamsburg. Beyond historic resources below ground, the Landmarks Commission and its successor, the Board of Historic Resources, recognized other well-known plantations and prominent public buildings such as county courthouses and city halls.[19] In 1976 the Jackson Ward Historic District in Richmond was granted official recognition, becoming the largest African American historic district in the nation.

In addition, VHLC members and staff gave talks and slideshows around the state and published *Notes on Virginia,* a broadly distributed journal that regularly lists new additions to the Virginia Landmarks Register and newly acquired easements on historic properties. In 1976 the first landmarks register book was produced, a hardbound volume containing a comprehensive list of properties enrolled as historic Virginia landmarks. This publication is now in its fourth edition.[20] Other

Jackson Ward National Historic District, Richmond, the largest African American historic district in the nation, is also recognized on both the National and Virginia landmarks registers. It includes buildings associated with African American business, religious, commercial, and residential life in the late nineteenth and early twentieth centuries. Some of its dwellings display the finest cast-iron work in the city. (Virginia Department of Historic Resources)

agency publications included *A Guidebook to Virginia's Historical Markers* (1984) by Margaret T. Peters, and *Landmarks of Black History* (1988) by Calder Loth. For thirteen years the VHLC sponsored a program of instruction about Richmond's architectural history for inner-city schoolchildren, a series that was adopted in several other localities.

A 1979 federal law providing income tax credits to those who restored their historic buildings involved the VHLC more deeply in building technology, and the commission served as an important clearinghouse for good preservation practices. The federal tax credits stimulated interest in programs like the Virginia and national registers, because historic landmarks that were "income producing" were eligible for tax credits. Federal income tax credits should not be confused with state preservation tax credits, which were not put in place in Virginia until 1999.

By the early 1980s the VHLC's workload had grown beyond the small agency's capabilities. Local governments were seeking the VHLC's guidance in developing local land-use plans, now that planning for historic resources was permitted under the *Virginia Code*.[21] Preservationists realized that the VHLC needed an organizational advocate to lobby for more funding and staff. Leaders of several state groups joined forces to form the Preservation Alliance of Virginia, comprising the Historic Staunton Foundation, the Association for the Preservation of Virginia Antiquities (APVA), the Historic Richmond Foundation, and the Waterford Foundation, formed by a group of Loudoun County residents to save the tiny Quaker village of Waterford from expanding development and skyrocketing land values in Northern Virginia.

In the spring of 1984 the first meeting of the new Preservation Alliance took place at Monticello, Thomas Jefferson's home in Albemarle County. Individuals, local historical societies, institutional organizations, local governments, and libraries were all invited to join. Although the VHLC had always had strong support from prominent individuals, it could now call upon this statewide lobbying group to speak for preservation interests in the political arena.

Regrettably, Virginia's entire environmental community suffered a serious blow in 1984 over an issue of historic preservation. The state had developed a long-range plan for Capital Square in Richmond and wanted to demolish the historic buildings it owned on East Main Street. Estimated costs to demolish the buildings did not reach the level that under state policy triggered an automatic environmental impact review, so the state believed it could proceed without regard to the historical value of the structures. In addition, although VHLC chair Mary Douthat Higgins had stated publicly that the buildings were significant, they had not yet been formally entered on the Virginia Landmarks Register.

Adjacent property owners in the Shockoe Valley, represented by the Shockoe Slip Foundation, filed a lawsuit alleging that the state had failed to consider its own policy to conserve its historic resources as articulated in its 1970 constitution. The legal question was whether the policy directives in the state constitution were "self-executing." Unfortunately, on January 18, 1985, the Virginia Supreme Court ruled that Article XI, section 1, was not self-executing, which meant that environmentalists could not depend on the language in the constitution alone to protect natural and historic resources from official state actions such as demolition.[22] The buildings were torn down and replaced with a state parking garage.

In 1988, David J. Brown, the Preservation Alliance director, persuaded Governor Baliles to authorize a formal study of historic preservation.[23] The first comprehensive evaluation of preservation of the built environment, the study recommended that the VHLC become a full-fledged department of the state government. A newly named Department of Historic Resources would carry out the same functions and retain the same mission, but it would be on a level with the Departments of Conservation, Transportation, Health, and Taxation in the hierarchy of state agencies. Its seven-member board would continue to be appointed by the governor and would retain its responsibilities to designate historic landmarks and accept preservation easements, just as the original Virginia Historic Landmarks Commission had done under the 1966 legislation. The General Assembly adopted the recommendation for the Department of Historic Resources in 1989, and Governor Baliles selected the former chief architect for the National Park Service, Hugh C. Miller, as its first director. George Freeman was appointed chair of a new Historic Resources Board under the new department.[24]

The state revolving fund was established in 1989 under the same legislation that elevated the historic VHLC to a state department. The revolving fund was used to buy historic buildings and resell them with protective perpetual easements. In 1999 administration of the fund was transferred to the APVA, and in 2005 the APVA, its focus having evolved from individual historic buildings to a far broader concern for historic districts and long-range preservation issues, merged with the Preservation Alliance of Virginia, the statewide preservation advocacy consortium. The new organization, APVA–Preservation Virginia, is now a powerful force for all aspects of historic preservation.[25]

The General Assembly expanded the preservation easement program later by requiring that historic properties receiving state grants of more than $50,000 be placed under a perpetual easement to the state. This requirement protects not only the landmark but also the public's investment in its preservation. The law limited these grants to local governments or qualifying nonprofit organizations. This led to protection of a far broader assortment of buildings: courthouses, theaters, train stations, and even churches. By the end of 2006 these grants had resulted in more than fifty Virginia historic buildings being placed under easement protection.[26] Easements now protect the nationally famous James River plantations of Westover, Berkeley, Shirley in Charles City County, and Tuckahoe, Thomas Jefferson's boyhood home in Goochland County. Private easements have been donated on a historic sheet-metal shop, a canal lockkeeper's house, tobacco factories, gristmills, historic taverns, Civil War earthworks, a general store, and an almshouse. Virginia's African American heritage is guarded by several easements, including Madden's Tavern in Culpeper County, Mount Moriah Baptist Church in Roanoke, the Dover Slave Quarter Complex in Goochland County, and some properties in the Jackson Ward Historic District in Richmond.

Virginia has secured, at minimal expense, permanent legal protection through perpetual easements of 425 privately and publicly owned historic places as of June 2007, representing the full spectrum of Virginia's history and culture. The Commonwealth can take great pride in its many citizens who have voluntarily elected to preserve important historic resources through the easement program. The value of these easements at the time at which they were given amounted to hundreds of millions of dollars. These tangible acts of stewardship enable a rich and irreplaceable cultural legacy to be passed intact to future generations.

An unfortunate, indeed outrageous, event occurred in 1992–93. Widespread growth in Northern Virginia had brought tremendous increases in land assessments. At the same time, a revived interest in saving historic Civil War battlefields conflicted with the inexorable development spreading from metropolitan Washington and Richmond. The Department of Historic Resources and its Historic Resources Board became convenient targets of attack by the foes of open-space and historic preservation. These groups charged the state with infringing on private property rights when it certified as "historic land-marks" the site of the large battlefield around Brandy Station in Cul-peper County, where on June 19, 1863, the largest cavalry engagement of the Civil War took place, as well as the somewhat smaller battlefield area at Bristoe Station in Prince William County, where on October 14, 1863, A. P. Hill suffered a disastrous defeat that ended Lee's attempt to cut off Meade's withdrawal from the Rappahannock to Washington. Property rights advocates contended that historic designations imposed hardships on owners who wanted to get top prices for their land, and that historic designation made their land less saleable. Despite the Vir-ginia Supreme Court's earlier ruling that listing on the Virginia Land-marks Register was only a "hortatory act," realtors, road builders, and developers rallied to persuade the General Assembly to change the existing law. The General Assembly obliged them, passing a bill that allowed landowners to block historical designation of their individual properties by filing a formal objection. The bill also allowed a majority of owners to block designation of a historic district for listing as a Vir-ginia landmark.[27] Complex notification procedures were incorporated into the legislation, which confused the process with zoning actions by local governments.[28] Angry editorials in several newspapers around the state supported the bill, particularly the *Richmond Times-Dispatch,* which castigated the Department of Historic Resources for overstep-ping its boundaries and trampling property rights. Passage of this leg-islation was also supported by well-heeled developers and lawyers who bussed in large contingents of angry landowners to demonstrate at the Capitol. Following unusually acrimonious debate, in which several en-vironmentally sensitive legislators strenuously opposed the proposed restrictions on the historical agency, the bill was adopted by both the Senate and the House and was signed by Governor Wilder. Its enact-ment defeated one of the major purposes of the original 1966 legisla-tion by undermining the value of the Virginia Landmarks Register as a nonregulatory honor roll of landmarks of intrinsic historic value.

During the same session, the General Assembly, again bowing to developers' pressure, passed another act removing those two Northern Virginia Civil War battlefields from the Virginia Landmarks Register. This was an unprecedented violation of the constitutional separation-of-powers principle and also showed blatant disregard of the facts. George Freeman, then chairman of the board, compared the General Assembly's fiat to Pope Paul V's ban, during the Inquisition, on denying that the sun revolved around the earth.[29]

Despite the deterioration and loss of historic buildings and neighborhoods, and regardless of confrontations about issues of property rights, the Department of Historic Resources continued its quest to save the body of manmade resources that embodies our shared history. It has provided oversight and guidance for the rehabilitation of hundreds of historic buildings through preservation tax credits, resulting in millions of dollars' worth of investment and revitalization of dozens of Virginia's cities and towns.[30] It has indeed taken off with a vengeance and assumed a life of its own. Unfortunately, it has often been forced to play the role of David to the Goliath of developers and their lawyers in the war between saving historic properties and the rich and powerful forces of urban growth and sprawl.

Virginia's Parks and Scenic Roads

B Y 1965, VIRGINIA already had some experience in developing recreation areas for state parks and in pursuing ways to enhance highway travel. Nearly forty years earlier, the Garden Club of Virginia, the
Virginia Academy of Science, and the Izaak Walton League had all
approached Governor-elect John Garland Pollard to express the need
for state parks. In the late 1920s, Virginia and Kentucky were already
working to establish an interstate park that would straddle their shared
boundary, and Tidewater residents were advocating a park on the Atlantic Ocean that would allow the public to enjoy pristine beaches.

Virginia's magnificent Shenandoah National Park and the George
Washington and Jefferson National Forests had a combined land area
of 1.4 million acres but were far away from the population centers east
of the Blue Ridge Mountains. Indeed, most federal parks and forests
were inaccessible to the public, both because of geography and also
because during the Great Depression and World War II many families
did not own automobiles, or if they did, they could not afford the gaso-
line to fuel them. By 1965, however, the state's population had grown
in both size and density, and accessibility to parks had become more
important. The demands for access also grew dramatically as more and
more people moved to suburban areas and were financially able to own
an automobile.

The Garden Club of Virginia had begun a crusade to beautify the

landscape back in the 1920s, when the automobile was starting to enable motorists to view Virginia's stunningly beautiful countryside as
they traveled new highways.[1] Garden Club members recognized that
ridding travel corridors of trash could encourage an appreciation for a
clean environment, so they lobbied to clean up litter and remove the
billboards that were already becoming an eyesore. No one under-
estimated the lobbying clout of the Garden Club of Virginia when it
visited the General Assembly to seek remedies.

Building new highways and making travel more enjoyable remained
high on the agenda of Virginia's political leadership into the 1930s. The
familiar historical markers along many secondary roads had their gen-
esis in 1926 legislation that called for historic sites in Virginia to be
identified and marked appropriately. Dr. H. C. Eckenrode was appointed to perform this task. The far lower highway speeds in those
days made the marker texts readable for the interested traveler. The
marker system thrived in the 1930s, and the ubiquitous markers still
abound along Virginia's roads.[2]

The acquisition of state parklands in the 1930s had been haphazard.
No state funds had been appropriated to buy land for that purpose and
there was no overall vision. President Franklin D. Roosevelt created the
Civilian Conservation Corps (CCC) in 1933, which undertook park
construction on six Virginia sites that had been acquired by the
Commonwealth for state parks. In 1934 the first chairman of the State
Conservation Development Commission, William Carson, aptly articulated the mission of a parks system, saying, "I would rather build a
park where the plain people of Virginia can spend a pleasant outing
and find pleasure and recreation close to nature than to build a great
church or endow a cathedral."[3] Even at that time, Virginia's fast-
disappearing wilderness worried thoughtful citizens who believed public outdoor recreation areas were important. On June 15, 1936, Virginia
became the first state in the country to open its entire park system all
at once. The inaugural parks were Seashore, now known as First
Landing (Virginia Beach); Westmoreland (Westmoreland County);
Staunton River (Halifax County); Douthat (Bath and Alleghany coun-

Stately cypress trees define First Landing State Park in the City of Virginia Beach. (Virginia Department of Conservation and Recreation)

ties); Fairy Stone (Patrick and Henry counties); and Hungry Mother (Smyth County).[4] All were immensely popular.

Over the next thirty years the state added only five additional parks to its system. All the land for the five new parks was given to the state, so that the only new state expenditures involved operation and maintenance costs. The largest of the new parks was Pocahontas State Park in Chesterfield County, donated to the state by the National Park Service in 1946. The land for Prince Edward State Park for Negroes was donated to the state in 1939. The park's name reminds us today that the state's segregationist policy often denied many of our fellow citizens equal access to our parks. The Hillsman House in Prince Edward County and other tracts around it were given to help create the 219-acre park at Sailor's Creek battlefield. The 327-acre park at Claytor Lake in Radford was purchased by citizens in the surrounding region, and given to the state in 1948. The Staunton River Battlefield Park was opened by the state on land donated by the United Daughters of the Confederacy in 1956. In the 1980s it was enlarged with eighty acres donated by Dominion Electric Coop and Virginia Power.[5]

Recognizing the potential of the parks as outdoor classrooms, park staff began to offer environmental programs to visitors, highlighting the natural wonders of the outdoors. Also, special areas were set aside as early as 1960 for scenic hiking on trails along shorelines and mountain ridges. Established state parks were not the only public outdoor recreation facilities in the state in the years preceding the publication of *Virginia's Common Wealth*. There were also "recreation areas" where people could hunt, fish, hike, and view wildlife, managed by the state's Game and Inland Fisheries Commission and the Forestry Division.

In 1965 the Virginia Outdoor Recreation Study Commission, chaired by FitzGerald Bemiss, stated in its report, "Outdoor recreation must involve state parks and the roads which take people to them."[6] Until then, Virginia had had no blueprint at all for providing outdoor recreation. Dennis Baker, a longtime state park employee and later the Parks Department director, has observed that the only thing keeping outdoor recreation projects going at all was a gentlemen's agreement that parks should be a public service. He believes that Bemiss's dream for expanding the state's commitment to state parks, and his efforts to sell that dream to the public, were instrumental in ultimately defeating fiscal conservatives who opposed any substantial state funding for parks.[7] Although the legislature in 1966 did not appropriate all the money sought by the VORSC, it did appropriate some funds that, when supplemented with money from the federal Land and Water Conservation Fund, were sufficient for five splendid new parks: Grayson-Highlands, Mason Neck, Natural Tunnel, False Cape, and York River.[8]

In 1974, Bemiss proposed to the Virginia legislature that the state purchase new land by selling $84 million in bonds. He was frustrated to find that he could not secure support for the proposal because legislators believed the economic climate was not right to issue bonds. After the state turned down the proposal, a diplomatic Bemiss was quoted in the Richmond press as saying, "I am disappointed that the political leadership doesn't see it as I do . . . but [they] have other people to deal with who have programs they feel just as strongly about as I do about mine."[9]

Bemiss and his VORSC colleagues also recognized that improvement of the roads that led to state parks was important, as were roads "of incomparable natural charm and historical significance." As they put it in their 1965 report, "Roads (and corridors) should be identified and developed for the general enjoyment of all Virginians."[10] The definition of a "byway" in state law incorporated the VORSC's thinking: "a road designated as such by the Commonwealth Transportation Board has relatively high aesthetic or cultural value, leading to or within areas of historical, natural, or recreational significance." Under the enabling law, preference for selecting official Virginia byways was to be given to corridors already protected by some sort of local zoning that preserved the "aesthetic or cultural value of the highway."[11] Virginia already had a great many scenic back roads, and giving them formal recognition and marking them for travelers proved to be a successful and popular program; more than three thousand miles of scenic drives across the Commonwealth were protected under the legislation. The state Department of Transportation explained that what made a byway different from other roads was that "people like to explore." A 2000 survey found that "driving for pleasure is the second most popular outdoor activity in Virginia with more than 62 percent of the population taking to the road for pure enjoyment."

By the time Bemiss completed his term on the VORSC in 1974, the public finally understood that parks were important to the physical health and lifestyles of Virginia's citizens. The state and local park programs had been improved and expanded, and a total of sixty-three grants had been made to help develop local and regional parks and thus supplement state facilities. During Bemiss's tenure, private property owners donated significant pieces of land that would later become state parks: Chippokes Plantation in Surry County (1967) from Mrs. Victor Stewart, and Caledon Natural Area in King George County (1974) from Ann Hopewell Smoot. The two-thousand-acre Caledon is a designated

Virginia scenic byway Route 130 takes the travelers through agriculturally rich Amherst County, Virginia. (D. Allen Covey, Virginia Department of Transportation)

national natural landmark with one of the largest concentrations of bald eagles on the East Coast.

There were four more additions to the state's park system through 1992. Sky Meadows, in the pristine Paris Valley in Fauquier County, was given by Paul Mellon in 1975. Leesylvania in Prince William County was made possible by a gift from the American-Hawaiian Steamship Company in 1979. The New River Trail, a gift from the Norfolk Southern Corporation in 1985, was an unusual park in its linear configuration, a plan mirrored by several localities using abandoned railroad rights-of-way in areas like Fairfax County and Rockbridge County. Designated a national recreation trail by the U.S. Department of the Interior, the New River Park stretches fifty-seven miles along the river in Grayson, Carroll, Wythe, and Pulaski counties, and includes two tunnels and three large bridges that offer hikers scenic river and mountain vistas. Kiptopeke State Park, created in 1992, is a 356-acre parcel located at the tip of Northampton County, the Eastern Shore's only state park. The purchase was paid for with funds from the Virginia Recreational

Facilities bond issue and acquired by the Trust for Public Land on behalf of the Commonwealth.

Virginia voters gave overwhelming support to a bond referendum in 1992 that provided substantial funding for expanding the state park and natural areas system. The funds were used to buy Belle Isle, a 733-acre park in Lancaster County; fifteen hundred acres in Buckingham County for James River State Park; the 190-acre Wilderness Road Park in Lee County in 1993; and the 1,604-acre Shenandoah River State Park, in Warren County[12] in 1994, as well as eleven new natural area preserves.[13]

Land for two small parks was acquired in 2006: High Bridge Rail Trail, another linear park donated by Norfolk Southern Corporation that runs through Nottoway, Prince Edward, Cumberland, and Appomattox counties, and Middle Peninsula State Park in Gloucester County, which was acquired from private owners using state funds.[14]

Today no Virginia resident lives more than an hour's drive from one

Virginia scenic byway Route 665 (Loyalty Road) winds through the countryside near the rural hamlet of Taylorstown in Loudoun County, Virginia. (D. Allen Covey, Virginia Department of Transportation)

Belle Isle State Park on the Rappahannock River in Lancaster County, Virginia, offers visitors a quiet respite. (Virginia Department of Conservation and Recreation)

of the thirty-four state parks or forty natural areas in the state. Parks encompass 62,338 acres and five hundred miles of trails that are open to the public.[15] In addition, 4,065 acres have been "land banked" and await final planning and funding. Nearly seven million visitors a year enjoy a range of recreational activities. Most of the state's parks offer overnight camping facilities, cabins, water recreation, historical exhibits, museums, and interpretive events. In 2001, Virginia was recognized as having the best-managed park system in the nation by the National Sporting Goods Association Sports Foundation, Inc.[16]

Meanwhile, the Garden Club of Virginia encourages the Department of Transportation to expand its wildflower program to beautify hundreds of miles of interstate highways, and continues to wage its decades-old struggle against billboards and highway litter. Scenic Virginia, formed in 1998 as a Virginia subsidiary of Scenic America, has promoted riverfront view shed preservation, municipal tree projects, and the designation of additional scenic byways.[17] Scenic America also offers technical assistance to localities to help "eliminate or prevent visual blight," such as cell towers and towering billboards. Billboards, always the nemesis of highway travel, are controlled on interstate highways in Virginia, and localities such as Fairfax, Loudoun, and Fauquier have forbidden them altogether on their primary roads, but the eighty-year-old battle over removing them altogether rages on in most localities.

Virginia is also blessed with a number of national historical parks that attract visitors from both the Commonwealth and around the nation. Fredericksburg, Richmond, Petersburg, and Manassas have Civil War battlefield parks with attractive interpretive centers in protected rural settings. The colonial national parklands at Yorktown and Jamestown have welcomed visitors for decades.

The authors of *Virginia's Common Wealth* saw state park expansion and operation as a moral obligation. But as the costs of maintaining parks and public areas increased, there was much debate over whether to provide park access as a public service or to charge fees. Some legislators today see the system as an "economic generator," as fees are charged for admission, parking, and use of all park facilities. Parks continue to be viewed as important tourist attractions—which they surely are—but their role in enhancing all Virginians' quality of life, regardless of their ability to pay, must not be overlooked in a culture more and more oriented to the "bottom line."

The Chesapeake Bay and Virginia's Rivers

THE JEWEL of Virginia's water resources is the Chesapeake Bay, the maritime centerpiece of the state. "Heaven and earth never agreed better to frame a place for man's habitation," as Captain John Smith put it in 1608.[1] The Chesapeake Bay is the largest estuary in the United States and one of the richest sources of seafood in the world. A member of a Japanese delegation visiting the Virginia Institute of Marine Science in Gloucester, Virginia, said, "If we had the Chesapeake Bay, we could feed the world." That visitor acknowledged that Japan did not have the mechanisms for cleaning it up, however. He went on to say that America was fortunate to have an outspoken public that supported preserving this remarkable resource, a public concern that was missing in his own country. The question of the past fifty years is to what extent Virginia's public concern and commitment have succeeded, and whether the maritime centerpiece of Virginia's natural resources will die.[2]

The Chesapeake Bay's watershed incorporates more than 64,000 square miles in six states and the District of Columbia. More than 15 million people live along its shores, and it is home to more than 2,700 species of plant and sea life. The Bay has been a primary transportation route for settlements in Virginia and Maryland since the seventeenth century. In Virginia alone there are 5,200 miles of tidal shoreline; Chesapeake Bay wetlands harbor more than 21,000 acres of sea grasses and 225,000 acres of vegetation, a critical spawning ground for hundreds of species.[3] Although all the mid-Atlantic states benefit from and are enhanced by the Chesapeake, the runoff from their contaminated soil pollutes the rivers that empty into it.

Virginia was one of the first states in the nation to enact its own water control law to combat water pollution from industrial and municipal wastewater discharges, which it did in 1946, two years before Congress adopted the first federal Water Pollution Control Act. The state has a history of paying attention to its valuable marine species that goes back to the 1800s. The Virginia Fish Commission was established in 1875, and in 1884 the Commonwealth set up the Board of the Chesapeake to regulate the oyster industry. In 1898 these two merged to form the Board of Fisheries, which was charged with managing both shellfish and finfish issues. The first mention of habitat protection within the state's waters appears in the 1902 constitution. Its provisions were carried over into the 1970 constitution in Article XI, section 3: "The natural oyster beds, rocks and shoals in the waters of the Commonwealth shall not be leased, rented or sold, but shall be held in trust for the benefit of the people of the Commonwealth, subject to such regulations and restrictions as the General Assembly may prescribe, but the General Assembly may, from time to time, define and determine such natural beds, rocks, or shoals by surveys or otherwise."[4] The drafters of the 1970 constitution added sections 1 and 2 to Article XI, establishing a Commonwealth policy to "conserve, develop and utilize its natural resources, its public lands, and its historical sites and buildings." The powerful state conservation efforts of the 1960s did not specifically address the ecological health of the Bay, because it still seemed invulnerable because of its magnitude.

The first environmentalists to address the Bay were a group of Baltimoreans who chartered a volunteer organization in Maryland in 1967. This was the Chesapeake Bay Foundation, which was to become a powerful political advocate for issues relating to the Bay. The new organization, led by Arthur Sherwood, was alarmed by the increasing number of boats, people, and houses on the Bay, not to mention sewage and industrial discharges. The foundation adopted "Save the Bay" as its motto and began printing the blue and white bumper stickers that are commonly seen throughout states that border the Bay. The foundation was headquartered in Annapolis and later opened offices in Virginia, Pennsylvania, and the District of Columbia as well.[5] The Virginia Environmental Endowment, headed by Gerald McCarthy, played a key role in establishing the Chesapeake Bay Foundation's Virginia office.

Not until the early 1980s, when a new leader in Virginia's environmental movement appeared on the scene, did Virginia begin to address the issues of a seriously polluted Chesapeake Bay. W. Tayloe Murphy Jr., a lifetime resident of Virginia's Northern Neck, grew up on the banks of the Rappahannock and Potomac rivers, and his childhood memories of the Chesapeake Bay and its tributaries inspired him to pursue the restoration and health of Virginia's natural resources. His devotion to environmental stewardship led him to follow his father—a state legislator—into public service, applying his skills as an attorney, a legislator, and finally as Governor Mark Warner's secretary of natural resources. His work for the environment reached across the state, but the Chesapeake Bay and its tributaries were always at the heart of his commitment.

In November 1981, Charles Robb was elected governor of Virginia, and Murphy was elected to the House of Delegates. He was appointed to the House Committee on Conservation and Natural Resources and the Committee on the Chesapeake and Its Tributaries when the House convened in January 1982. In that year's General Assembly session he cosponsored a resolution, with delegates Harvey Morgan of Gloucester County and Robert Bloxom of the Eastern Shore, directing the Joint Legislative Audit and Review Commission (JLARC) to examine the economic potential and the management of Virginia's seafood industry. The JLARC is an agency of the Virginia legislature that studies issues likely to be of broad public concern and therefore subject to future legislation.

During Murphy's first session as a member of the House, he was appointed by the speaker to a vacancy on the Chesapeake Bay Commission, a bi-state commission created by joint legislation of Maryland and Virginia in 1980. At the first meeting he attended as a member,

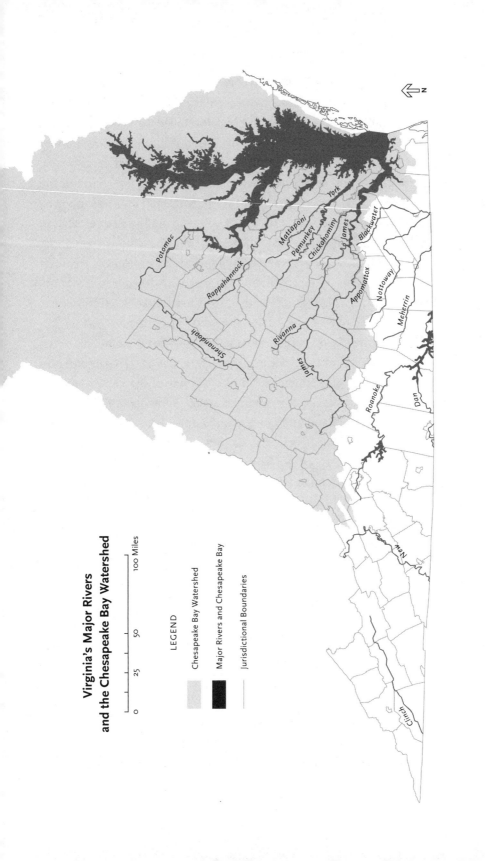

Virginia's Major Rivers
and the Chesapeake Bay Watershed

0   25   50   100 Miles

LEGEND

Chesapeake Bay Watershed

Major Rivers and Chesapeake Bay

Jurisdictional Boundaries

Potomac

Rappahannock

Shenandoah

Mattaponi

Pamunkey

Chickahominy

York

James

Rivanna

James

Blackwater

Appomattox

Nottoway

Meherrin

Roanoke

Dan

New

Clinch

N

later that year, the commission received a briefing on the contents of a forthcoming report on the Chesapeake Bay by the U.S. Environmental Protection Agency (EPA). The EPA had developed this 1982 report over a ten-year period following the agency's establishment in 1970, under legislation sponsored by Senator Charles Mathias of Maryland.

The EPA report identified the problems affecting the health of the Bay, the primary one being that nutrient (nitrogen and phosphorus) overenrichment and toxic substances entering the Bay had resulted in a huge loss of submerged aquatic vegetation. As soon as the Chesapeake Bay Commission received the report it began to plan a conference of the states bordering the Bay to seek ways to address the problems. These plans led directly to the 1983 Chesapeake Bay Conference, held at George Mason University in Fairfax, Virginia.

The George Mason conference marked the start of an official intergovernmental effort to rescue and protect the Bay and its tributaries—the Chesapeake Bay Initiative. On the last day of the conference the historic Chesapeake Bay Agreement was signed by Governor Robb, the governors of Maryland and Pennsylvania, the EPA administrator, and the chair of the Chesapeake Bay Commission. By signing the agreement Governor Robb bound Virginia to take action with its neighbors. They were later joined by the mayor of the District of Columbia, which is located in the Chesapeake Bay watershed and has a stake in its health comparable to that of the three governors.

These signers and their successors now constitute the membership of the Chesapeake Bay Executive Council, the governing board of the multi-jurisdictional Chesapeake Bay Program headquartered in Annapolis. Governor Baliles himself served as chair of the executive council and in that capacity initiated the effort to rewrite the Chesapeake Bay Agreement of 1983. As a result of his leadership the council adopted the 1987 agreement, under which the Bay program operated until 2000, when the current agreement was adopted.

In 1985, Virginia, Maryland, and Pennsylvania adopted joint legislation by which Pennsylvania became a full member of the Chesapeake Bay Commission, thereby increasing its membership to twenty-one: five legislators from each state, one citizen member from each state, and a designee by the governor of each state to make up the executive branch on the commission. The chairmanship of the commission rotates annually among the three states. During his eighteen years on the commission as a legislator, Tayloe Murphy served as its chair in 1988, 1991, and again in 1997. During his four years as secretary of natural resources he served as Governor Warner's designee to the commission.

Murphy later wrote, "If it had not been for that Conference at George Mason, we wouldn't have had the Bay program (and the Commission to oversee its implementation); without the Commission we would never have had the institutionalized framework to implement the 1983 Bay Agreement."[6]

One of Murphy's early speeches to the Virginia Seafood Council so impressed U.S. Representative Herbert Bateman of Newport News that Bateman asked that it be published in the *Congressional Record*. The speech addressed the entire range of serious threats and challenges to the health of Chesapeake Bay. Murphy's conclusion read:

> On a more tangible but equally important level, protection of the Bay
> has become a goal that transcends philosophical and political
> boundaries . . . there is no "conservative" or "liberal" or "Republican"
> or "Democratic" position on the Bay's place as a national treasure,
> or in the importance of restoring and maintaining it for ourselves and
> our posterity. The Bay is so important and its plight so obvious, that it
> has become one of those rare subjects that generates almost automatic
> consensus.[7]

But Murphy recognized that although the consensus was real, the details, or the costs, of acting on that consensus were the challenge.

As Gerry Bemiss and his colleagues had said in *Toward A New Dominion: Choices for Virginians*:

> We are convinced that most Virginians stand behind the Common-
> wealth's declared policy. At the same time, we find that many of our con-
> servation programs are neither appropriately designed nor adequately

funded. As our natural resource problems increase in complexity and potential danger, we seem ill-prepared to move swiftly and surely to prevent irreparable damage.

Our inertia may be due, in part, to the very richness of our natural resources heritage: great rivers providing water for every need; the Chesapeake Bay full of oysters, crabs and rockfish; clean air and clean water, and right at hand for all to enjoy, the lovely and productive Virginia countryside. We are lulled by this agreeable landscape and assume it is safe now and assured for all the years to come. (Emphasis added.)[8]

Virginia's environmental leaders were fully committed to saving the Bay, but they also were aware of the required costs and the predictable opposition. Fiscal conservatives could be expected to object to the monetary costs, and political conservatives would object to any restraints on the uses of private property through zoning changes. Even as the Virginia's Future report assigned top priority to restoration and perpetual care of the Chesapeake Bay, it noted that most earlier local government efforts had run afoul of a body of court decisions thwarting efforts to expand zoning powers. Between 1955 and 1978, says the report, "the Virginia Supreme Court heard seventeen cases challenging land use actions of cities and counties on the grounds that they were extending their zoning powers beyond those granted by the General Assembly. In all but one of those cases, the court invalidated as unauthorized by law the innovative exercises of zoning powers. . . . Political determinations about individual land use should not be interfered with, even by local government."[9]

Not, apparently, even when a valuable state resource was at risk. It had become abundantly clear that pollution from roads, industrial and residential development, shopping centers, and other construction was having a disastrous impact on the quality of the Chesapeake Bay. Yet to limit uses of its immediate shoreline to protect the Bay was considered absurd public policy.

Governor Robb's term ended before he and the legislature could follow up on the environmental portions of the Virginia's Future report, but his successor, Gerald L. Baliles, made passage of the Chesapeake Bay Preservation Act the cornerstone of his environmental program for the 1988 session of the General Assembly. This was the most significant legislative initiative to date in Virginia's efforts to save the Bay. Governor Baliles, having prosecuted many polluters as attorney general from 1981 to 1985, campaigned vigorously for expanding the state's oversight of development along river banks in order to protect the Chesapeake Bay.

In 1988, Joseph H. Maroon became the Virginia executive director of the Chesapeake Bay Foundation. A veteran of the Water Resources Research Center at Virginia Polytechnic Institute and State University (Virginia Tech), he had headed the JLARC study of the Virginia seafood industry. Maroon, with his strong background in conservation and water quality issues and his years at JLARC, understood the machinations of state government. He worked closely with Tayloe Murphy, who had come to personify and represent the Bay's interests, both in the Virginia General Assembly and as an effective and passionate public spokesman.[10]

The Chesapeake Bay Preservation Act of 1988 established a new citizen regulatory board called the Chesapeake Bay Local Assistance Board and a new state agency called the Chesapeake Bay Local Assistance Department. The former was charged with requiring all localities in Tidewater Virginia to enact ordinances compelling riverside landowners to construct buffers to filter out pollutants from "nonpoint-source run-off."[11] The latter was established to assist localities in adopting and implementing their ordinances. Governor Baliles appointed James C. Wheat to serve as the first chairman of the Chesapeake Bay Local Assistance Board on the theory that his prominence in state political and business circles would "give pause" to anyone who might be skeptical about the importance of the new Bay legislation.[12]

Wheat had also served on the Chesapeake Bay Land Use Roundtable created in 1986 through an appropriation to the Chesapeake Bay Commission. Senator Joseph Gartlan and Delegate Tayloe Murphy were the commission's representatives to the roundtable, which was facilitated by the Institute for Environmental Negotiation at the University of

Massive commercial and residential development mars the landscape on the banks of the Chesapeake Bay. (© Dave Hartcorn, davidhartcorn.com)

Virginia. The recommendations contained in the roundtable's report, issued in December 1987, were incorporated into the provisions of the Chesapeake Bay Preservation Act.[13] The Virginia Environmental Endowment provided ongoing funding to the Institute for Environmental Negotiation so that it could facilitate the complex mediation that led to the Chesapeake Bay Preservation Act and the Chesapeake Bay Local Assistance Board.

The 1988 Chesapeake Bay Preservation Act, which came to be known simply as the Bay Act, was the basis for most subsequent laws relating to the Bay's environmental health. A JLARC report summary of 2002 says that the act established a "partnership between the state and eighty-four of Virginia's easternmost localities located in the Chesapeake Bay watershed while not unduly restricting the rights of landowners to develop their property." It directed the state to provide financial and technical assistance to help localities enforce new land-use requirements, a particularly significant commitment because local governments always complained that the state issued far too many "unfunded mandates."[14]

According to Tayloe Murphy, state environmental agencies and local governments have been reluctant to step boldly into the gap to define "unreasonable use of private property." In most instances, he maintains, Virginia has "adhered to a concept of property rights that is not at all compatible with the public trust doctrine."

Many environmentalists wanted the Bay Act to apply to nontidal wetlands as well as tidal ones, but the word came down that this was asking too much, too soon. In the political climate of 1988, it was not yet possible to convince non-Tidewater residents that they might be responsible for a body of water as distant as the Chesapeake Bay, even though the idea had been around for more than twenty years.

Murphy sees his appointment to the commission as the most essential reason for his effectiveness as a spokesman for the environment in

A working farm on the Chesapeake Bay has appropriate vegetation and trees screening the fields from the Bay. (© Dave Hartcorn, davidhartcorn.com)

succeeding years. Since 1982, he says, "the problems haven't changed much, and in many cases they have just gotten worse."[15] Nutrient over-enrichment, toxic substances entering the Bay, and loss of submerged aquatic vegetation continue to plague the Chesapeake today. Although the Bay jurisdictions have programs in place to address these problems, there has never been enough financial support from the states and the federal government to implement the programs fully.[16] The early promise of regional cooperation notwithstanding, the goal of a healthy Chesapeake Bay has not been reached in the quarter-century following this auspicious beginning.

Part of the Chesapeake Bay's waterways, of course, consist of Virginia's rivers, most of them rising in the mountains and flowing east-southeast to the Atlantic Ocean or west-southwest into the Tennessee and Ohio river basins. Several—the Potomac, the James, the York, and the Rappahannock—flow directly into the Chesapeake Bay. The river waters themselves, and their watersheds, are loaded with pollutants, and all contribute hugely to the Bay's contamination. The James River watershed alone covers some ten thousand square miles, or nearly 25 percent of the state.[17]

Public concern for Virginia's rivers centered on preserving their natural beauty and exploiting their outdoor recreation potential, until 1965, when the Virginia Outdoor Recreation Study Commission expressed its alarm in *Virginia's Common Wealth*: "It is increasingly clear that the present demands on Virginia's rivers—their waters and their shorelines—require comprehensive river basin research and planning to conserve our most vital resources."[18]

The Scenic Rivers Act of 1970 finally acknowledged the importance of the ecological health of Virginia's rivers. Even though its primary purpose was the "identification, preservation and protection of certain rivers that possess natural beauty of high quality," its goal was to see that the rivers were protected for "their scenic, recreational, geologic, fish and wildlife, historical, cultural and other values."[19] But awareness of their pollution was growing.

Then, in 1972, the U.S. Congress passed the federal Water Pollution

Control Act. When amended in 1977, this body of federal law became commonly known as the Clean Water Act. The Clean Water Act initially targeted "point-source pollution," or pollution whose source was either single or multiple identifiable locations or industries. Point-source pollution included waste from municipal treatment facilities and industrial sites that often contained dangerous by-products and other pollutants. Two of these point-source pollutants were Allied Chemical's discharge into the James River of kepone, a toxic chemical used in making pesticides, and phosphate, a chemical found in many cleaning agents.

In 1976 concerned landowners along the James River between Richmond and Newport News formed the Lower James River Association (LJRA). The Virginia Environmental Endowment provided funding in 1983 that enabled the LJRA to hire its first staff. Initially the LJRA limited its efforts to educational programs about the river's history and its importance to local landowners. But in 1983 it hired a professional staff and embarked on a more aggressive political agenda. In addition to lobbying for improved water quality laws and stronger state legislation to protect the Chesapeake Bay, it underwrote a study evaluating all existing water resource legislation. The resulting report urged state administrative agencies to use tools already contemplated by the VORSC—voluntary conservation easements and historic district designations.[20]

The LJRA worked with the Richmond and Crater planning district commissions to explore ways in which localities could comply with the Clean Water Act, focusing particularly on the city of Richmond, which was one of the biggest contributors to James River pollution. Richmond, whose combined sewer overflow system was outdated and inadequate, was ordered to comply with ever more stringent state and federal water quality standards. One uncooperative legislator introduced a bill to exempt Richmond from fish passage requirements around the numerous dams blocking the James within the city limits. Environmentalists fiercely opposed the bill, and the LJRA managed to broker a compromise, giving the city a short extension to build the fish passages, a solution that benefited people as well as the fish.[21]

But valuable as these moves were in filtering and removing pollut-ants from municipal waste, they did nothing to address the most damaging pollutants—those from "nonpoint" sources—farms, con-struction sites, and road-building projects. The dramatic increase in nitrogen- and phosphate-laden chemical fertilizers used on farms as well as on suburban lawns and golf courses, and the tremendous loss of natural vegetation to developers' bulldozers, not to mention parking lots, interstate highways, roads, and streets, are a devastating setback to the Bay's natural filtering system.

As Virginia enacted legislation to comply with the sweeping Clean Water Act, it again became a model for other states. Virginia's legisla-tion required that all companies in the state provide a toxic substance inventory, and the law carried penalties for noncompliance. Nitrogen and phosphorus in particular pollute river and Bay water alike, causing algae to grow out of control, which limits the water's capacity to breathe, thus harming and killing the shellfish and finfish populations. In an initial move to address the phosphorus issue, Congress adopted the Phosphate Detergent Act in 1987, which prohibited the use of most phosphate cleaning agents, but the ban had limitations, and enforce-ment was difficult. And it did nothing to address the use of chemical fertilizers.

Effective action on this issue meant confronting both fiercely inde-pendent farmers and the very powerful developers' lobby. Persuading farmers to change their methods so as to reduce damage to rivers and wetlands is difficult work. Convincing developers of the need to cut down on density and include open-space buffer zones is equally chal-lenging. "Leading without control" is how Joseph Maroon described the job of the state's conservation agencies.

By then, moreover, the Virginia Supreme Court had already dealt a blow to natural resource conservation and historic preservation, when in 1985 it held that the environmental protection policies articulated in the 1970 constitution were not "self-executing."[22] This meant that en-vironmentalists could not expect the constitution alone to protect natu-ral and historic resources from official state actions—the governor and the General Assembly would have to step in to implement this policy.

As a growing scholarly community produced increasingly sophisti-cated analyses of water pollution, its causes, and possible solutions, conservationists in government, business, and nonprofit groups were gaining ever higher levels of education and professional preparation. There was a revolution in thinking about fisheries science as the twenty-first century began, with scientists at the Virginia Institute for Marine Science, part of the College of William and Mary, leading the way. Whereas the study and management of marine life in the Bay and its tributaries had in the past focused on single species, the new empha-sis was on the complete picture: the real-world interaction of predator-prey relationships, habitat conservation, wetlands protection, and pol-lution prevention. VIMS researchers, funded by almost $700,000 of Virginia Environmental Endowment grants over five years, have re-defined the approach to fisheries planning and management. Unfor-tunately, though, the general public has not kept up in its understand-ing of the extremely fragile ecosystem that comprises the Chesapeake Bay and its rivers and streams.

Virginia has the legal framework to protect its water resources. Over the past three decades the Commonwealth has begun to work with other states to address the difficult issues associated with cleaning up a huge, irreplaceable body of water. Virginia also has in place the programs needed to address both the point and nonpoint sources of pollution. What it lacks is the political will to appropriate the necessary funds. Until Virginia's leaders, public and private, treat the protection of the environment as a core responsibility of government—federal, state, and local—and give conservation the same weight as education, law enforcement, health care, and the other functions of government, the quality of our water, land, and air resources will continue to decline.

More and more, enlightened leaders and citizens have realized that the Chesapeake Bay cannot be considered in isolation. Nearly two-thirds of the state is responsible for the problems of the Bay; the water-sheds draining into the Bay cover that much territory. The difficulty lies in convincing political leaders and their constituents that some per-sonal freedoms and property rights must be sacrificed for the common good. Road builders, transportation planners, farmers, property owners, and development moguls have had to endure restrictions to one degree or another, and will continue to have to, a fact that has met with considerable resistance. Virginia is blessed with cadres of volunteers committed to saving the Bay—the Chesapeake Bay Foundation, the James River Association, the Garden Club of Virginia, and hundreds of others whose only recompense is that they are on the side of the angels in this struggle.

The question facing Virginia now is whether public concern will motivate public and private policymakers and individual citizens to salvage the health of the Bay, which has been allowed to deteriorate to such a serious degree. It is now a question of life or death.[23]

Afterword

VIRGINIA'S *COMMON WEALTH* articulated the historic and open-space conservation ethic, although its triumphant promise was not always fulfilled in the succeeding decades. The absorption of the Virginia Historic Landmarks Commission into a larger Department of Natural Resources during the Robb administration was a setback that fortunately was remedied by the General Assembly during the Baliles administration. The redefinition of the powers of the Virginia Council on the Environment during the Allen administration was a much greater setback, and one that has never been reversed. It continues to inhibit full consultation and coordination among state agencies on major actions affecting the environment.

Various special interest groups have continued to try and weaken these laws in other ways. Localities have been unable to afford, or unwilling to implement, some of the VORSC's recommendations. Individuals have been leery of regulations or restrictions on their use of their lands. And most damaging of all, some governors and legislators have had higher priorities for the appropriation of state funds. Thus, while there have been successes, there also have been many setbacks and failures. The most notable of the failures is the state's unwillingness to honor its commitments under the Chesapeake Bay Compact. Next to that are the General Assembly's recent amendments weakening the Virginia tax-credit program. They have cast a black cloud of uncertainty over the state's heretofore booming open-space easements program. This in turn has forced potential easement grantees to make difficult, and potentially counterproductive and unfair, choices as to priorities among willing donors. Because of different land-use patterns in different parts of the state, the Virginia Outdoors Foundation, for example, now gives priority to gifts of easements on one hundred or more acres. This policy discriminates against small landholders and riverside landowners in the Tidewater and favors large farms and timber tracts in the Piedmont, the Shenandoah Valley, and Southside.

With the hindsight of the forty-two years since Virginia first focused on its responsibility to protect its environment and historic resources, what have we learned, or forgotten?

It is difficult to answer this question abstractly. So I have tried to put it in perspective by identifying what I believe are the most severe failures of Virginia's current government that pose immediate threats to our environment and our way of life.

First and foremost is the state's continuing failure to provide the means necessary for compulsory comprehensive regional planning. Despite the multiple shortcomings of our antiquated local governmental structure, we continue to leave it in place. It has no counterpart in any other state in the Union and is unique in its inefficiency and parochialism. Virginia needs to go back to where the Metropolitan Areas Study Commission Report of 1967 (the "Hahn Commission" report) left off. We need to face up to the fact that its halfway nonsolution of voluntary regional planning districts has not solved the pressing problems still facing our metropolitan areas. They will only be resolved by consolidating the core city of a metropolitan area with its surrounding urban and urbanizing counties into a single metropolitan local government.

Second, we still do not adequately plan for, or provide our fellow citizens with in a timely way, an efficient public transportation system. Such a system would include more than safe and efficient highways and roads. There also must be adequate mass transit within our metropolitan areas. In addition, we need efficient rail connections with our neighbors in the East Coast megalopolis. Western Europe today is light years ahead of us in providing efficient rail travel for its people within their cities and countryside.

Beyond these two major failures, which cry out for correction, there are other clouds over Virginia's open-space conservation and historic preservation programs. They are (1) the Virginia General Assembly's continuing reluctance to adequately fund its agencies working for those goals; (2) the unknown effects of the 2006 cutbacks in Virginia tax credits for private landowners who donate conservation easements on their properties for open space or historic preservation; (3) the lands heretofore thought to be protected by "perpetual" conservation easements under Virginia law, which now face the threat of destruction, thanks to the federal Energy Policy Act of 2005, for the sake of corridors for electric power lines to serve privately owned, for-profit power grids. At present in Northern Virginia, proceedings at both the federal and state level have pitted ever-increasing electricity needs against the protection of our ever-dwindling environmental and historic resources. Fortunately, lands protected by perpetual open-space easements under the Virginia Open Space Land Act by the Virginia Outdoors Foundation, the Virginia Board of Historic Resources, and other Virginia public bodies afford substantial protection from this threat.[1] And (4) balancing private property rights with protecting the public's best interests. Under existing law it sometimes appears that the real estate developers get all the breaks. On other occasions, the hard-working builders seem to be swamped by regulations and special ordinances.

There is still room for hope. Looking to the future in anticipation of the ever-increasing pressures of population and development on Virginia's remaining open space, the recommendations set forth in *Virginia's Common Wealth* in 1965 must be updated, and the public good put above private profit. In addition, our lawmakers must rise above partisan rivalry and ideological differences and must make, and then keep, a long-term commitment to providing the funds necessary for buying land for additional state parks and acquiring ecologically important natural areas. The state must also provide financial aid to regions and localities for acquisition of land for parks and open space. Finally, the General Assembly must carefully examine the consequences of its

2006 constraints on landowners' tax credit incentives for post-2006 gifts of scenic and historic easements and make certain that they are not crippling the state's most effective means of protecting open space—voluntary landowner generosity.

Perhaps the best way to get Virginia back on the right track is for the governor to do what Governor Harrison did in 1965 and create a blue-ribbon commission to look at the current state of conservation, historic preservation, and badly needed mandatory regional planning. Only in this way can we get a clear view of where we are headed, and determine what we need to accomplish if we are to realize a new vision for the Commonwealth of Virginia.

FitzGerald Bemiss
Richmond, Virginia
October 2007

Appendix A

Virginia's State Parks by County and Year Established

State Park	Counties	Established
Bear Creek Lake	Cumberland	1940
Belle Isle	Lancaster	1994
Breaks Interstate	Dickenson	1954
Caledon Natural Area	King George	1985
Chippokes Plantation	Surry	1967
Claytor Lake	Pulaski	1951
Douthat	Alleghany, Bath	1936
Fairy Stone	Henry, Patrick	1936
False Cape	City of Virginia Beach	1969
First Landing	City of Virginia Beach	1933
George Washington Grist Mill	Fairfax	1936
Grayson Highlands	Grayson	1965
Highbridge	Cumberland, Prince Edward, Nottoway	2006
Holliday Lake	Appomattox, Buckingham	1938
Hungry Mother	Smyth	1936
James River	Appomattox, Buckingham, Nelson	1999
Kiptopeke	Northampton	1992
Lake Anna	Spotsylvania	1972
Leesylvania	Prince William	1978
Mason Neck	Fairfax	1967
Middle Peninsula	Gloucester	2006
Natural Tunnel	Scott	1971
New River Trail	Carroll, Grayson, Pulaski, Wythe	1986
Occoneechee	Mecklenburg	1944
Pocahontas	Chesterfield	1962
Powhatan	Powhatan	2003

State Park	Counties	Established
Raymond R. "Andy" Guest, Jr.		
Shenandoah River State Park	Warren	1994
Sailor's Creek Historic Battlefield	Amelia, Prince Edward	1937
Seven Bends	Shenandoah	2007
Shot Tower	Wythe	1964
Sky Meadows	Clarke, Fauquier	1975
Smith Mountain Lake	Bedford	1967
Southwest Virginia Historical		
Museum	Wise	1946
Staunton River	Halifax	1936
Staunton River Battlefield	Charlotte, Halifax	1936
Twin Lakes	Prince Edward	1939
Westmoreland	Westmoreland	1936
Widewater	Stafford	2006
Wilderness Road	Lee	1993
York River	James City	1969

Appendix B

Conservation Easements in Virginia by Jurisdiction

Jurisdiction	Total acres	Number of easements	Jurisdiction	Total acres	Number of easements
Accomack	13,941.15	60	City of Galax	50	1
Albemarle	65,941.85	364	City of Hampton	0	0
Alleghany	4,449.57	8	City of Hopewell	0	0
Amelia	265.8	2	City of Lexington	8	1
Amherst	2,418.43	19	City of Lynchburg	0	0
Appomattox	411.99	2	City of Manassas	100	5
Arlington	15.99	20	City of Newport News	15	3
Augusta	11,121.52	91	City of Norfolk	0	0
Bath	15,806.24	50	City of Petersburg	405	8
Bedford	3,933.33	24	City of Portsmouth	0	0
Bland	1,015	2	City of Radford	149	2
Botetourt	5,031.05	55	City of Richmond	3	58
Buckingham	467.03	2	City of Roanoke	131.04	5
Campbell	3,160.52	10	City of Salem	3	1
Caroline	3,341.58	15	City of Staunton	259	4
Carroll	1,051.72	8	City of Suffolk	291.89	6
Charles City	2,979.49	13	City of Virginia Beach	365.69	12
Charlotte	1,799.67	4	City of Waynesboro	0	0
Chesterfield	511.03	8	City of Winchester	115.27	6
City of Alexandria	9.36	19	Clarke	17,777.59	161
City of Bedford	56.92	7	Craig	3,412.26	18
City of Charlottesville	1	4	Culpeper	7,995.11	36
City of Chesapeake	680.71	6	Cumberland	329.15	4
City of Colonial Heights	1	1	Dinwiddie	104	3
City of Danville	73.15	1	Emporia	0	0
City of Franklin	9	2	Essex	5,513.5	22
City of Fredericks	233.47	9	Fairfax	815.65	44

Jurisdiction	Total acres	Number of easements	Jurisdiction	Total acres	Number of easements
Fauquier	70,423.55	451	Northumberland	991.362	22
Floyd	3,788.46	30	Nottoway	275.05	1
Fluvanna	8,058.02	17	Orange	23,650.24	120
Franklin	3,129.02	24	Page	949.92	13
Frederick	3,008.777	22	Patrick	917.01	6
Giles	3,063.57	16	Pittsylvania	739.62	9
Gloucester	844.69	14	Powhatan	1,647.57	6
Goochland	2,061.66	18	Prince Edward	917.81	8
Grayson	4,066.59	30	Prince George	2,610	3
Greene	6,459.14	39	Prince William	1,023.98	18
Halifax	1,707	5	Pulaski	2,213.5	14
Hanover	1,549.48	16	Rappahannock	24,960.01	164
Henrico	246	6	Richmond	3,827.36	22
Henry	155.56	3	Roanoke	2,697.08	22
Highland	4,638.65	14	Rockbridge	18,958.5	127
Isle of Wight	42	3	Rockingham	2,421.93	19
James City	562	13	Russell	10,626.59	11
King and Queen	4,307.95	20	Scott	925.38	11
King George	3,259.33	18	Shenandoah	2,975.68	30
King William	6,602.83	21	Smyth	1,073.19	5
Lancaster	991.07	12	Southampton	721.16	4
Lee	331.74	2	Spotsylvania	3,725.79	25
Leesburg	120	1	Stafford	2,632.29	18
Loudoun	26,786.89	333	Stafford County	70	1
Louisa	5,349.72	23	Surry	458.5	5
Lunenburg	484.03	2	Sussex	869.47	3
Lynchburg	39	1	Tazewell	14,618.37	7
Madison	8,182.25	55	Warren	6,337.7	64
Mathews	349.25	6	Washington	2,827.77	10
Mecklenburg	49	4	Westmoreland	5,908.16	23
Middlesex	1,211.74	8	Wise	96.47	3
Montgomery	9,669.66	50	Wythe	2,382.95	13
Nelson	7,722.13	35	York	285.5	3
New Kent	331.5	3			
Northampton	10,346.88	78	*Totals for the State*	521,968.769	3,411
Northamton	123	2			

Appendix C

Real Property in the Urban Society

FitzGerald Bemiss

By now it is hackneyed to observe that Virginia is changing from a rural-agricultural state to an urban-industrial state. There is still enough novelty in the situation to cause us to repeat the statement, and there is just enough evidence of the change to cause us to agree. But we are a long way from realizing the extent of the metamorphosis and even further from tooling up to take charge of and attempt to direct the new energy which is being generated in Virginia.

The intriguing thing about the present state of Virginia's change is that it appears to have brought to us many benefits of urbanization and industrialization without yet having inflicted upon us their full costs and penalties. As our personal incomes have increased we have adjusted our standard of living upward. This has frequently cost us more than our income, but installment credit has "solved" this problem. But we are only beginning, more or less unconsciously, the upward adjustment of the standards of living of our local and state governments. First we buy the fancy new car and *then* we want better roads to drive it on. We buy the suburban ranch house and *then* want the schools, playgrounds and libraries. We are now in the latter stages of the lag between the gratification of private desires and the gratification of public desires, which involve everything from more neighborhood police to bigger and better universities, mental hospitals and highways.

In this stage, we begin to see, but do not face up to, the conflict between our preference for the least possible government confined to the smallest possible units, and the obvious need for more efficient, orderly and centralized governmental structures. Our responses are frequently cut to get the job done without really changing anything. The State has increased its budget, but so far mainly out of growth and minor adjustments rather than adoption of a major new tax system. Suburban counties, blessed with prosperous, problem free young people, subdivisions and shopping centers, provide inescapable services like sewers and schools through bond issues and defer other services to maintain the fiction of high living on low taxes. Let the next generation face the tough problems of reclamation and rehabilitation when the full impact of unplanned "development" really hits. And even the central cities which have acquired all the costly services and problems have until just recently been able somehow to absorb them; suddenly they are being driven to enact local sales taxes to balance their budgets.

CITIES BURDENED

The burdens of Virginia's cities are very real and are common to the core of every growing metropolitan area. Here, as higher income families depart for the suburbs, lower income families come from rural areas, frequently with little education and no technical skills. They cannot find jobs; they and their ample families consume a full range of community services while contributing little to their cost. Not only must the central city do the job of schooling, welfare, health, law enforcement, for this segment, but it must maintain an accessible and alluring downtown if for no other reason than to retain the businesses of the executives who live in suburbia and the shopping trade of their wives. To a great degree, the high standards of a city are set by these non-residents.

The rural counties, in many cases having lost their agricultural economic base, have had to turn more and more to the State for financial assistance, particularly in their principal area of service—public education. Two-thirds of the rural counties now receive over 50 percent of their revenues from State funds. Still, this has not gone far enough to dispel completely the illusion of sovereign independence which a good many of those counties maintain, nor has it substantially interfered with the long established county political and governmental structure

PROGRAMS BEGUN

But something has to give pretty soon. In fact, it is already giving. The State, having committed itself to the economic complex of the eastern seaboard, has to educate young people up to the economic and social standards of that complex. It has to have a positive and competitive program of intelligent conservation and development of its natural, social and economic resources. There is fairly general agreement on this and we appear to be willing to adopt a state-wide sales tax to accomplish it. Rural counties are stirring not just for more aid but for industries, technical schools, community colleges and even in some cases better management, land use plans and improved assessment and tax collection methods. Suburban counties are submitting to some small degree of metropolitan regional planning and beginning to provide at least enough services to protect themselves in annexation suits.

A by-product of all this is a new and peculiar political alignment. In past years, within State politics there were simply two groups—city boys and country boys. Within the generally conservative Virginia political context the city boys were considered less conservative and the country boys more conservative. The city boys had entered the Social Contract and had become reconciled, and in some cases even enthusiastic, about government services. The country boy, on the other hand, lived in a state of general self-sufficiency and maintained his position in government by being against government—and against city boys. This has changed. The city boy has not just submitted to the Social Contract, but has become keenly aware that a major metropolitan community simply cannot make the grade without an alert and active government supplying a full range of first-rate services. The country boy, no longer self-sufficient and independent, is now largely dependent on the State's program of school aid and on Federal farm and rural development programs. So these two groups, so long at opposite poles, now find themselves together on one significant point: that is, that they know they can't get along without government. I hasten to say that this doesn't mean that they like it particularly, but they see that they must have more money for the services which their constituents are demanding and that it has to come from somewhere.

SUBURBS DENY

The new citadel of conservatism is now suburbia. Here is a land populated mainly by a generation which has known only post–World War II prosperity— no major wars and no major depressions. Here is the best of two worlds, close to the services, amenities and economic advantages of the central city, but relatively free of government. Suburbia still lives within the lag, denying its dependence on the central city. Perhaps no real damage has been done by any of these situations as they now exist. But obviously the lag cannot be perpetuated, plunging as we are into urbanism. There is great peril in a static attitude toward a dynamic condition. Nothing could be more important than for Virginia to reckon reasonably with the urban condition. But within the urbanizing area the division of philosophies and expectations along totally irrelevant boundary lines creates a stalemate between the central city and suburbia; and the subdivisions are like two men being swept over a cascade as they argue about which seat they are going to occupy in the canoe. Virginians have looked with dread and scorn on the impacted urban centers of the east. But we are daily creating, probably for ourselves and certainly for our successors, these very conditions. Is there really any reason why we should be spared from these costly urban difficulties unless we plan and act to direct our growth toward qualitative results as well as quantitative ones? Living as we do at the foot of the volcano, like the citizens of Pompeii, we can indeed be sealed in and smothered by the ash of urban eruption. The metropolitan area, including the central city and its suburban satellites, is in fact a single economic and social unit. To pretend that individual political subdivisions are like sovereign islands scattered through the vast reaches of the South Pacific is a fantasy which we cannot afford, and which will effectively prevent us from dealing positively with the urban opportunities and hazards.

STATE GOVERNMENT CHALLENGED

It becomes clearer and clearer that where two or more political subdivisions share a common resource or a common problem, they simply cannot expect to solve the problem separately; they most solve it together. But as recent merger and acquisition experience has indicated, there is little likelihood that the components of these emerging metropolitan areas will form themselves voluntarily into constituencies appropriate to the problems of the area. Occasionally they work out a mutually satisfactory answer to a sewage disposal problem or to a traffic problem, but generally only the rawest edges of the large common problems are dealt with and these only under the pressure of some sort of crisis.

Knowing that local governments are "creatures of the State," students of government have for many years argued that there should be consolidations of small rural counties into sizes and shapes more nearly attuned to the 20th century conditions. Though unquestionably desirable from a practical and economic point of view, consolidations in these quarters is of trivial importance compared to that of adjusting the constituencies of major metropolitan areas to the problems of major metropolitan areas, and of breaking the stalemate which prevents the development of unified urban policies and programs for the sensitive advancement of the entire community. An example of what happens in this state of affairs is the unplanned, uneconomical abuse and consumption of urban land. It is unnerving to think what the next generation is going to say about us when it sets about unsnarling the traffic problems, removing the substandard and ill-designed housing developments, reconstituting the water tables, reclaiming park lands and financing rehabilitation projects that will dwarf today's urban redevelopment programs.

COOPERATION NECESSARY

In conclusion—we are committed to progress. This means we are committed to the urban condition and its assets and its liabilities. Though we are momentarily enjoying more assets than liabilities, we will, unless we give intelligent guidance to our new energy, come to a condition in which we have more liabilities than assets. This will be the real and critical testing ground of the validity of state government in the near future. In fact, the response of state governments to the challenge of urbanization is likely, within very few years, either to reestablish the state government as a working partner in our total system of government, or to reduce it finally to a mere performer of ceremonial and housekeeping functions. When Vice-President Humphrey recently invited the mayors of American cities to pick up the phone and call him about their problems, he stated a clear challenge to state government. If the state allows the central cities to secede and take their allegiance to Washington, it will be spelling its own doom. It appears then that Virginia must abandon the whimsy and clutter of present annexation procedures and take a positive hand in shaping its subdivisions so they can live and perform in the specialized urban-industrial complex, more effectively developing their capacity to serve the entire state. This would be first among many steps toward restoring the balance of capacities and powers between state and federal government so vitally important to our total governmental structure.

This article was originally published in the *Virginia Law Weekly*, vol. 17, no. 6 (1965).

Notes

1. The Historical Backdrop

1. *The Statutes at Large, being a collection of all the Laws of Virginia from the first session in the year 1619*, 13 vols. (Charlottesville: University Press of Virginia, 1969), 1:59.

2. *U.S. Antiquities Act, U.S. Code* 6 (1906), §§431–33.

3. See http://www.cr.nps.gov/history/online, the official Web site of the National Park Service.

4. The National Park Service had twenty categories of national park properties, including such historical sites as Civil War battlefield parks at Manassas, Spotsylvania, Richmond, and Fredericksburg, and such areas as Assateague National Seashore. Shenandoah is Virginia's only true "national park," in the same category as Yellowstone, Acadia in Maine, and Smoky Mountains in Tennessee and North Carolina.

5. See http://www.nps.gov/state/va/.

2. The Vision and the Beginning

1. Others present at this meeting were Mrs. Bocock's sister, Mary Ross Scott Reed, and her son, William T. Reed III. The Conservancy chapter was formally organized at another meeting at Mrs. Bocock's house, on November 16, 1960, at which they and many others were present. See *The Virginia Chapter, the First 40 Years*, a publication of The Nature Conservancy's Virginia chapter.

2. "Bemiss to Head Commission on Recreation Facilities," *Richmond Times-Dispatch*, June 30, 1964.

3. "An Act to Create the Virginia Outdoor Recreation Study Commission," March 31, 1964, *Acts and Joint Resolutions of the General Assembly of the Commonwealth of Virginia*, extra session 1963, regular session 1964 (Richmond: Department of Purchase and Supply, 1964), chapter 277, §147, p. 485.

4. The commission's other members were A. Plunkett Beirne, James L. Camblos, Walther B. Fidler, Cecil F. Gilkerson, Mrs. Meriwether Lewis, Paul W. Manns, Floyd K.

McKenna, George N. McMath, Dorman M. Miller, Meade Palmer, and Stockton H. Tyler. Ex officio members were Douglas B. Fugate, commissioner of the Virginia Department of Highways; Chester F. Phelps, executive director of the Commission of Game and Inland Fisheries; and Marvin M. Sutherland, director of the state's Department of Conservation and Economic Development. Particularly fortuitous was the choice of John O. Simonds, of the landscape architectural and planning firm Simonds and Simonds of Pittsburgh, as consultant to the VORSC. "Bemiss to Head Commission on Recreation Facilities," *Richmond Times-Dispatch,* June 30, 1964.

5. *Beauty for America: Proceedings of the White House Conference on Natural Beauty* (Washington, D.C.: U.S. Government Printing Office, 1965), Introduction.

6. Bill Sauder, "Action to Preserve Coast Marshes Urged," *Richmond Times-Dispatch,* January 7, 1965.

7. Quoted in "Permanent State Agency Proposed to Develop Recreation Resources," *Richmond Times-Dispatch,* January 7, 1965.

8. Alexander, Jennings, and Nichols were later appointed by Governor Harrison to the first Virginia Historic Landmarks Commission. Ibid.

9. Quoted in "Bemiss Urges Regional Approach," *Richmond Times-Dispatch,* February 1, 1965.

10. Charles Houston, "Natural Beauty Talk Urged in Virginia," *Richmond News Leader,* May 27, 1965.

11. Quoted in Virginia Churn, "More Pleasant Roads Are Urged," *Richmond News Leader,* February 11, 1965.

12. George Freeman, VORSC special counsel, later served as special counsel to the committee that drafted this federal legislation.

13. "Water Resources Group Is Named," *Richmond News Leader,* October 6, 1965.

14. *Beauty for America,* 1.

15. Quoted in Adam Berstein, "Laurance Rockefeller Dies at 94," *Washington Post,* July 12, 2004, B4.

16. Laurance Rockefeller to FitzGerald Bemiss, February 4, 2002, in FitzGerald Bemiss's possession.

17. FitzGerald Bemiss, conversation with author, May 2006.

18. Virginia Outdoor Recreation Study Commission, *Virginia's Common Wealth: A Study of Virginia's Outdoor Recreation Resources and the Virginia Outdoors Plan for Conserving and Developing Them for the Lasting Public Benefit* (November 1, 1965), Library of Virginia, Richmond.

19. Allan Jones, "Outdoor Recreation Plan for Virginia Is Proposed," *Richmond Times-Dispatch,* November 7, 1965, A1; editorial, "A Challenge to Virginia," ibid., November 8, 1965.

20. "A Comprehensive Plan Outlined for Park Development in Virginia," *Roanoke Times,* November 7, 1965, A6.

21. Charles Houston, "Natural Beauty Talk Urged in Va.," *Richmond News Leader,* May 27, 1965; "Beautification Meeting Called by Governor," *Richmond Times-Dispatch,*

August 27, 1965; Charles Houston, "Virginia's Beauty Conference Topic," *Richmond News Leader,* December 9, 1965.

22. See Virginia's 1972 constitution and the Virginia Supreme Court opinion in *U.S. v. Blackman,* 270 Va. 68, 613 S.E. 2d 442 (2005).

23. The Land and Water Conservation Fund (LWCF) was designed to provide assistance to states in the planning, acquisition, and financing of recreation lands. The bill was signed into law on September 3, 1964, and for the first time in the nation's history public funds were made available to states for that purpose. Previously, lands for parks and open space had to be either purchased directly by a government agency with public funds or acquired through private gifts and donations. Funds for the LWCF were to come from the sale of surplus federal property, motorboat fuel taxes, and fees imposed for recreational use of federal lands. The demands on the LWCF increased, and to meet the growing demand, funds from offshore mineral-leasing receipts were added to the fund. Although the value of the fund has fluctuated over the years, dropping to zero in 1982 and in the late 1990s, in 2000 some funding was restored, although never to the level reached at its height in 1979. The state recreation grants program remains the only LWCF program that "ensures the protection of America's resources in perpetuity." See "Land and Water Conservation Fund Program," http://www.tpl.org/, the Web site of the Trust for Public Land.

3. Milestones, 1966–1976

1. Virginia Outdoor Recreation Study Commission, *Virginia's Common Wealth: A Study of Virginia's Outdoor Recreation Resources and the Virginia Outdoors Plan for Conserving and Developing Them for the Lasting Public Benefit* (November 1, 1965), 86–96, Library of Virginia, Richmond.

2. A. E. Dick Howard, interview by author, March 25, 2006. Howard was executive director of the Commission on Constitutional Revision.

3. Elbert Cox (1906–93) was the first director of the Outdoor Recreation Commission. Cox served for more than thirty years with the National Park Service and was regional director of its southeast region from 1951 to 1966. Charles B. Hosmer, *Preservation Comes of Age: From Williamsburg to the National Trust* (Charlottesville: University Press of Virginia, 1981).

4. Max Ailor, "$3.5 Million Sought to Buy Land, Improve State Parks," *Richmond Times-Dispatch,* August 5, 1966.

5. Ibid.

6. From 1967 to 1977, The Nature Conservancy acquired fifteen tracts for Mason Neck State Park and Mason Neck National Wildlife Refuge totaling 2,970 acres, which were transferred to the Commonwealth and the federal government, respectively. The Conservancy acquired another tract for Mason Neck in 1987. Information provided by Michael Lipford of The Nature Conservancy.

7. FitzGerald Bemiss, conversation with author, April 2006.

8. William H. Lucy and David L. Philips, *Metropolitan Sprawl in Virginia: City Decline, Suburban Transition, and Farmland Loss, a Summary Report* (Charlottesville: University

of Virginia, Department of Urban and Environmental Planning, Commission on Population Growth and Development, 1994).

9. Virginia Metropolitan Areas Study Commission, *Metropolitan Virginia: A Program for Action* (1967), Library of Virginia, Richmond.

10. *Virginia Code* (1968), v. 224, §15.2-4203.

11. Other members of the commission included U.S. District Court judge Albert V. Bryan Jr.; Virginia Supreme Court justice George M. Cochran; chief judge of the U.S. District Court for the Western District of Virginia Ted Dalton; former president of the University of Virginia and former congressman Colgate W. Darden Jr.; Virginia Law School dean Hardy Cross Dillard; state court judge Alexander H. Harman Jr.; Richmond civil rights attorney Oliver W. Hill Sr.; president of the Virginia State Bar Sloan Kuykendall; president of the College of William and Mary Davis Y. Paschall; and future U.S. Supreme Court justice Lewis F. Powell.

12. A. E. Dick Howard, telephone interview by author, March 25, 2006.

13. Howard had been introduced to politics as a student when he worked with George Freeman for Bemiss's first state senate campaign in 1959.

14. A. E. Dick Howard, *Commentaries on the Constitution of Virginia*, 2 vols. (Charlottesville: University Press of Virginia, 1974), 2:1140.

15. Clive Duval (1912–2002) was an "ardent proponent of environmental conservation," according to his obituary in the *Arlington Connection*, February 26, 2002.

16. A. E. Dick Howard, "State Constitutions and the Environment," *Virginia Law Review* 58, no. 2 (1972): 196.

17. George Freeman, interview by author, June 15, 2007.

18. Gerald McCarthy, interview by author, April 4, 2006.

19. Former governor A. Linwood Holton, telephone interview by author, June 26, 2006.

20. FitzGerald Bemiss, conversation with author, April 2006.

21. Freeman, interview.

22. McCarthy, interview.

23. Hamilton Crockford column, *Richmond Times-Dispatch*, June 20, 1970.

24. Joseph Maroon, director of the Department of Conservation and Recreation, interview by author, May 2006.

25. Holton, interview.

26. John Hanes, personal communication, November 2006.

27. Holton, interview. The Historic Falls of the James Act provided for the creation of a nine-member advisory committee, with five members appointed by the governor. For example, the original advisory committee included Pete Anderson, John Bishop, George Freeman, Eleanor Hankins, Bob Hicks, John Pearsall, Tony Perrine, David Roszell, and R. B. Young. Louise Burke was appointed to the City Planning Commission, and its chairperson, Dr. R. B. Young, was elected the first chair of the advisory committee, a position he held for thirty years. In 1984 the Historic Falls of the James Act was amended to provide full state scenic river designation to the Falls of the James. The Scenic River Advisory Committee became the Falls of the James Scenic River Advi-

sory Board, with the same membership and method of appointment. In both phases of the board's history, the City of Richmond has been the administrative agency for this segment of the Virginia Scenic Rivers System, Inc. This represents greater local involvement than is found with most of Virginia's scenic rivers, which are administered solely by the Department of Conservation and Recreation (DCR). Richard Gibbons, environmental program manager of the DCR, has provided continuing support to the advisory board.

28. Holton, interview.

29. *Land Use Policies, Interim Report of the Virginia Advisory Legislative Council to the Governor and the General Assembly of Virginia*, House Document 14 (1973), 5.

30. See John Moeser and R. M. Dennis, *The Politics of Annexation—Oligarchic Power in a Southern City* (Cambridge: Harvard University Press, 1982), 142–88.

31. *Bradley v. Richmond School Board*, 416 U.S. 696 (1974).

32. *Virginia Acts of Assembly*, 2004 regular session, vol. 2, chapter 877, pp. 1355–63.

33. "Kepone a Chemical Disaster in Hopewell, Virginia," *International Journal of Health Sciences* 13, no. 2 (1983): 227–46.

34. McCarthy, interview.

35. Executive order no. 29 (1982), "Creating Governor's Commission on Virginia's Future."

36. Freeman's principal client under the Clean Water Act was the Utility Water Act Group. See Elizabeth H. Haskell, *The Politics of Clean Air: EPA Standards for Coal-Burning Power Plants* (New York: Churchill Livingstone, 1982), 17–18, 34–37, 39, 106.

4. OPEN-SPACE LAND CONSERVATION

1. Today this is a protected site in the national park system.

2. *Virginia Code*, §10.1-1701.

3. See Virginia's 1972 constitution and the Virginia Supreme Court opinion in *U.S. v. Blackman*, 270 Va. 68, 613 S.E. 2d 442 (2005).

4. George C. Freeman, interview by author, March 28, 2006. For detailed information on the underlying legal basis for conservation and preservation easements, see "Brief Amici Curiae of Historic Green Springs, Inc., Association for the Preservation of Virginia Antiquities, Inc., et al.," record No. 042404 (February 24, 2005), in *U.S. v. Blackman*.

5. *Virginia Code*, §10.1, 1800.

6. Ibid., chapter 22.

7. Tyson Van Auken and Clifford Schroeder, interview by author, May 2006.

8. "Bull Run Mountain rates high priority. This attractive mountain is closer than any similar resource to the metropolitan center." Virginia Outdoor Recreation Study Commission, *Virginia's Common Wealth, A Study of Virginia's Outdoor Recreation Resources and the Virginia Outdoors Plan for Conserving and Developing Them for the Lasting Public Benefit* (November 1, 1965), "Proposals for State Parks," 25, Library of Virginia, Richmond.

9. Personal files of George C. Freeman.

10. G. F. Fleming, A. C. Chazal, K. M. McCoy, and C. S. Hobson, *A Natural Heritage Inventory of VOF Properties on Bull Run Mountain* (Richmond: Virginia Outdoors Foundation, 1999).

11. Information about the Piedmont Environmental Council in the following paragraphs was provided by the PEC.

12. The nine counties were Albemarle, Clarke, Culpeper, Fauquier, Greene, Loudoun, Madison, Orange, and Rappahannock.

13. Listed on the Virginia Landmarks Register, June 6, 2007.

14. Virginia Landmarks Register, http://www.dhr.virginia.gov/.

15. Proceedings before the Federal Energy Regulatory Commission and the Virginia Conservation Commission pending as of August 2007, and notes from the Piedmont Environmental Council.

16. The information about The Nature Conservancy in this and succeeding paragraphs was provided by Michael Lipford, director of The Nature Conservancy in Virginia, in June 2007. The information is based on his personal and official files and recollections.

17. Information from the files of George C. Freeman and Michael Lipford.

18. Information from the files of Michael Lipford.

19. Michael Lipford, interview by author, April 6, 2006.

20. "Civil War Preservation Trust Rescues 1300 Acres of Hallowed Ground in 2006," http://www.civilwar.org/.

21. Information provided by Wendy Musumeci, easement coordinator for the Virginia Department of Historic Resources, June 20, 2007. For more discussion of the protection of Civil War battlefields, see chapter 5.

22. See http://www.dgif.state.va.us/about, the Web site of the Virginia Department of Game and Inland Fisheries.

23. See Appendix B for a tally of conservation easements in Virginia.

24. *Virginia Code*, §15.2-4301 et seq.; §15.1-1507 (1977); §10.1-1106 (1997) (state forester directed to encourage general conservation of forested tracts).

25. Governor's Commission on Virginia's Future, *Toward a New Dominion: Choices for Virginians* (December 1984), 94, Library of Virginia, Richmond.

26. Thomson Gale, publisher, *Environmental Encyclopedia* (2003), www.bookrags.com/research/james-g-watt-1938—american-former—enve-02/, accessed June 24, 2008.

27. *Virginia Code*, §10.1-1009-1010 (definitions of "conservation easement," "holder," "public body," etc.).

28. "The readily apparent purpose of the Virginia Conservation Easement Act (VCEA) was to codify and consolidate the law of conservation easements to promote the granting of such easements to charitable organizations. When so viewed, it is clear that the VCEA did not create a new right to burden land by a negative easement in gross for the purpose of land conservation and historic preservation. Rather, it facilitated the continued creation of such easements by providing a clear statutory framework under which tax exemptions are made available to charitable organizations devoted to those purposes and tax benefits and incentives are provided to the grantors of such easements. The fact

that such easements were being conveyed without these benefits and incentives prior to the enactment of the VCEA does not support Blackman's contention that these easements were invalid at that time. To the contrary, Virginia not only was committed to encouraging and supporting land conservation and the preservation of historic sites and buildings in the Commonwealth, as evidenced by the constitutional and statutory expressions of that public policy discussed supra, but also recognized negative easements in gross created for these purposes as valid in 1973. Indeed, as noted by the district court, the granting of conservation easements by the landowners in the Historic Green Springs District was the direct result of the encouragement by the Governor for the express purpose of preserving the historic and natural beauty of that unique area. For these reasons, we hold that the law of Virginia in 1973 did recognize as valid a negative easement in gross created for the purpose of land conservation and historic preservation." *U.S. v. Blackman*, 81–82.

29. Lipford, interview.

30. Statistics provided by David Boyd, Virginia Department of Conservation and Recreation; Noel Harrison, National Park Service; and Wendy Musumeci, easement coordinator for the Virginia Department of Historic Resources, October 2007.

5. Historic Preservation

1. The Virginia Historical Society declared in an essay entitled "On This Day: Legislative Moments in Virginia History" (2004) that the bill "recognized Virginia's valuable historical resources. . . . The legislation sought to protect, preserve, and promote the irreplaceable tangible heritage of the Commonwealth." http://www.vahistorical.org/.

2. *With Heritage So Rich* (New York: Random House, 1966) served as a rallying cry for the preservation of buildings, sites, and historic districts across the nation. The foreword was penned by Mrs. Lyndon B. Johnson. Its call to action included many of the elements that appeared in the National Historic Preservation Act of 1966, the enabling legislation for the federal government's preservation programs.

3. Inspired by an article in the *Southern Churchman* about the collapse of Powhatan's Chimney in Gloucester County, Mrs. Galt suggested to Norfolk mayor Barton Myers the formation of a preservation society for Virginia's landmarks modeled on the Mount Vernon Association. She solicited support from her friends in Richmond and Williamsburg, and the organizational meeting for the Association for the Preservation of Virginia Antiquities was held in Williamsburg on January 4, 1889. See James M. Lindgren, *Preserving the Old Dominion—Historic Preservation and Virginia Traditionalism* (Charlottesville: University Press of Virginia, 1993), 42–43, 46.

4. See ibid., 91–94, for a detailed description of this transaction.

5. See the Colonial Williamsburg Foundation's Web site, http://www.history.org/Foundation/.

6. Junius R. Fishburne Jr., former director of the Virginia Historic Landmarks Commission (1972–76), telephone interview by author, June 21, 2006.

7. Alexander's scholarly credentials are attested by his earlier service as director of the State Historical Society of Wisconsin and director of the New York State Historical

Association. Dr. Alexander had been particularly instrumental in establishing the American Association for State and Local History in 1940. Charles B. Hosmer, *Preservation Comes of Age: From Williamsburg to the National Trust, 1926–1949* (Charlottesville: University Press of Virginia, 1981), 64, 86.

8. Statistics provided by Harry Hubbard, archivist for the Department of Historic Resources, July 2007.

9. Calder Loth, "Forty Years of Preservation: Virginia's Easement Program," *Notes on Virginia* 49 (2005): 49–54. Loth is the senior architectural historian at the Department of Historic Resources and has been involved with the easement program for many years.

10. Information provided by George C. Freeman, June 2007.

11. See, for example, *William Taliaferro Thompson et al. v. Douglas B. Fugate et al.,* 347 F.Supp 120 (U.S. District Court for the Eastern District of Virginia, Richmond Division, 1972). This case involved the National Historic Landmark property Tuckahoe, in which the court ruled in favor of the landowner against the Virginia highway commissioner and the U.S. secretary of transportation, holding that "condemnation of the property could not occur until the state and federal government had complied with all applicable federal laws, and thus granted the landowners' motion and denied the motion of the Highway commissioner and the Secretary of Transportation." This case involved the Highway Department's seeking to condemn some of the Tuckahoe property to construct Route 288 through Goochland County.

12. Background information in *U.S. v. Blackman,* 270 Va. 68, 613 S.E. 2d 442 (2005), upon questions of law certified by the U.S. District Court for the Western District of Virginia, opinion by Justice Lawrence L. Koontz Jr., June 9, 2005.

13. Stanley W. Abbott (1908–75) was a landscape architect with the National Park Service who designed the Blue Ridge Parkway and was its first superintendent. He later became superintendent of the Colonial National Historic Park in Williamsburg/Jamestown, Yorktown.

14. *VHLC v. Louisa County Board of Supervisors,* 217 Va. 468 (1976).

15. Fred Fisher, assistant attorney general of Virginia, conversation with author, March 2006.

16. But when federal funds are being used for a project or a federal permit being sought, the federal agency granting whatever actions are required to carry out that project must explore all feasible alternatives to see if the project might have an adverse effect on a property that is either officially listed on the National Register of Historic Places or has been found *eligible* for such a designation. Being listed or eligible for listing in the National Register cannot *stop* a federally funded or permitted project, but it does ensure that all alternatives are examined before the federal project can proceed. In common usage, this is known as "the environmental review process." However, under a ruling by Judge Robert R. Merhige in *Thompson et al. v. Fugate et al.,* the state was prohibited from carving out portions of state highway projects and funding them with state money just to avoid having to comply with federal environmental laws. If *any*

federal money pays for any portion of a highway project, the entire project is determined to be a *federal* project.

17. *U.S. v. Blackman.*

18. Ivor Noël Hume is a world-renowned archaeologist and author of the book *Here Lies Virginia: An Archaeologist's View of Colonial Life and History* (New York: Knopf, 1970).

19. For a discussion of all the courthouses and city halls in Virginia that are listed or eligible for listing on the Virginia Landmarks Register, see John O. Peters and Margaret T. Peters, *Virginia's Historic Courthouses* (Charlottesville: University Press of Virginia, 1995). In addition to the individual buildings listed on the Virginia and National registers, there are 524 historic districts, encompassing nearly 86,000 buildings, 3,000 structures, and 879 "objects," such as sculptures, monuments, etc.

20. Subsequent editions of the *Virginia Landmarks Register* were published by the University Press of Virginia in 1984 and 1999. All buildings and districts that have been registered are listed on the Department of Historic Resources Web site at http://www.dhr.virginia.gov/.

21. *Virginia Code* (1973), §15.2-2306.

22. *Cases Decided in the Supreme Court of Virginia,* vol. 228, September, October, and November 1984 sessions and January 1985 session (Richmond: Supreme Court of Virginia, 1984–85), 678–79. Additional information provided by Robert A. Carter, community services manager, Virginia Department of Historic Resources.

23. David Brown is currently executive vice president of the National Trust for Historic Preservation.

24. Calder Loth, *The Virginia Landmarks Register,* 4th ed. (Charlottesville: University Press of Virginia, 1999), x.

25. Elizabeth Kostelny and Louis Malon of the APVA–Preservation Virginia, interview by author, April 2006.

26. Information provided by the Department of Historic Resources.

27. Later incorporated into the *Virginia Code,* §10.1-2200 et seq.

28. The language that described the notification process was pulled from the section of the code that spells out notice requirements for zoning actions that can be taken only by a local government, not the state. While zoning actions do place restrictions on land use, historical designation does not. Also, the new law sponsors insisted that a "public hearing" be held prior to consideration of historic districts, again an action that was confusing, because a "public hearing" usually calls for those who appear at the hearing to give their statements under oath. Previously, the public meetings were informational only, allowing the state agency—in this case the Department of Historic Resources—to provide information about the historic resources and to explain the process for historical designation.

29. George C. Freeman, conversation with author, August 15, 2007.

30. See the journal *Notes on Virginia,* vols. 47, 48, and 49, for updates on the historic rehabilitation tax program in Virginia (2003–6). In 1999 the General Assembly enacted legislation that allows owners of historic properties to claim substantial tax credits for

rehabilitating their buildings in accordance with standards spelled out by the National Park Services for good preservation practices. Unlike the federal preservation tax credits, the state credits apply to both income-producing buildings and owner-occupied buildings. This program has been highly successful, resulting in millions of dollars' worth of sensitive rehabilitation projects and the revitalization of hundreds of urban commercial centers and neighborhoods across the state.

6. VIRGINIA'S PARKS AND SCENIC ROADS

1. Virginia had a reputation for good highways, which were particularly high on the political agenda of Governor Harry F. Byrd in the mid-1920s.

2. Scott David Arnold, comp., *A Guidebook to Virginia's Historical Markers*, 3rd ed. (Charlottesville: University of Virginia Press, 2007), xii–xiv.

3. Quoted in "Parks Improving at Record Pace," *Richmond Times-Dispatch*, June 11, 2006, J2.

4. Because of the distinctive building styles and landscaping associated with them and the history of the CCC, all of the original state parks have been designated historic landmarks. http://www.dhr.virginia.gov/.

5. Information provided by the Department of Conservation, June 2006.

6. The resolution to set up the Bemiss study that led to *Virginia's Common Wealth* reads, "Whereas there is constantly increasing demand for outdoor recreation facilities and constantly decreasing open space for providing those facilities . . . and whereas it is recognized that adequate outdoor recreation facilities are vital to Virginia's general and happiness and social and economical development . . ." *An Act to Create the Virginia Outdoor Recreation Study Commission*, chapter 277, approved by the Virginia General Assembly, March 1964.

7. Dennis Baker, interview by author, June 2006.

8. For a complete list of state parks in Virginia, see Appendix A. See also Katherine Calos, "Remember the Time When . . ." *Richmond Times-Dispatch*, June 11, 2006, J1.

9. Claude Burrows, "Lack of Interest in Bonds Scored," *Richmond News Leader*, February 14, 1974.

10. Virginia Outdoor Recreation Study Commission, *Virginia's Common Wealth: A Study of Virginia's Outdoor Recreation Resources and the Virginia Outdoors Plan for Conserving and Developing Them for the Lasting Public Benefit* (November 1, 1965), 88, Library of Virginia, Richmond.

11. "Virginia Byway defined," *Virginia Code*, §33.1-63 (1966, 1970, 1984, 1989).

12. The official name of the park is the Raymond R. "Andy" Guest, Jr. Shenandoah River State Park.

13. Records provided by the Department of Conservation and Recreation, June 2006.

14. A general obligation bond for parks and natural areas in 2002 also passed by 67 percent of voters, the same margin of victory as in 1992.

15. See "Virginia State Parks," http://www.dcr.state.va.us/parks/.

16. Information provided by Steve Hawks of the Department of Conservation and Recreation.

17. Scenic Virginia is headquartered in Richmond and works for the conservation of scenic beauty in the state.

7. THE CHESAPEAKE BAY AND VIRGINIA'S RIVERS

1. John Smith, *History of Virginia: The Travels, Adventures and Observations of Captain John Smith in Europe, Asia, Africak and America beginning about the yeer 1593 and continued to this present 1629*, 2 vols. (London, 1629; reprint, Richmond: Franklin Press, 1819), 1:114.

2. Joseph Maroon, director of the Virginia Department of Conservation and former director of the Chesapeake Bay Foundation, interview by author, April 28, 2006.

3. VMRC Management Highlights, "Habitat Management Overview," http://www.mrc.state.va.us/.

4. Web site of the Virginia Marine Resources Commission, http://www.mrc.state.va.us/.

5. See http://www.cbf.org/, the official Web site of the Chesapeake Bay Foundation.

6. Quoted in *Milestones—Chesapeake Bay Commission Annual Report* (Annapolis, Md.: Chesapeake Bay Commission, 2005), 26.

7. Tayloe Murphy, speech delivered before the Virginia Seafood Council in Williamsburg and reprinted at the request of Rep. Herbert Bateman in the *Congressional Record* 131 (April 16, 1985), 99th Cong., 1st sess., 1479–81.

8. Governor's Commission on Virginia's Future, *Toward A New Dominion: Choices for Virginians* (1984), 27.

9. Ibid., 35.

10. Maroon, interview.

11. Nonpoint-source runoff "comes from many diffuse sources. It is caused by rainfall or snowmelt moving over and through the ground. As the runoff moves, it picks up and carries away natural and human-made pollutants, finally depositing them into lakes, rivers, wetlands, coastal waters, and even our underground sources of drinking water." U.S. Environmental Protection Agency, http://www.epa.gov/, accessed September 24, 2007.

12. Former governor Gerald Baliles, telephone interview by author, June 24, 2006.

13. The Chesapeake Bay Preservation Act was adopted by the Virginia General Assembly in 1988. *Virginia Code*, §10.1-2100–2115 (1989).

14. Joint Legislative Audit and Review Commission, "Implementation of the Chesapeake Bay Preservation Act," October 15, 2002, Library of Virginia, Richmond.

15. Tayloe Murphy, interview by author, June 2006.

16. Ibid.

17. Information provided by the Lower James River Association.

18. Virginia Outdoor Recreation Study Commission, *Virginia's Common Wealth: A Study of Virginia's Outdoor Recreation Resources and the Virginia Outdoors Plan for Con-*

serving and Developing Them for the Lasting Public Benefit (November 1, 1965), 15th recommendation, Library of Virginia, Richmond.

19. Frits van der Leeden, *Water Atlas of Virginia* (Lexington, Va.: Tennyson Press, 1993); Scenic Rivers Act, *Virginia Code* §10.1-414.

20. Lower James River Association, *The Lower James River Watershed: Strategies for Resource Protection and Sustainable Development* (Richmond: Lower James River Association, December 1991).

21. Patricia Jackson, former director of the Lower James River Association, interview by author, March 2006.

22. *Robb v. Shockoe Slip Foundation,* 228 Va. 678, 324 S.E. 2d 674 (1985).

23. Maroon, interview.

Afterword

1. Energy Policy Act of 2005, section 216(b), http://eei.org/industry_issues/electricity _policy; *Virginia Code* §10-1-1704. See also Frederick S. Fisher (special assistant attorney to the attorney general of Virginia), "Condemning Protected Open-Space Land: Perspective of the Virginia Outdoors Foundation"; and George Clemon Freeman Jr., "An Update on Virginia Law Applicable to Possible Destruction of 'Perpetual' Easements on Historic Properties and Open Space by Condemnation—It All Depends upon Who Is the Grantee," papers delivered at the *Virginia Environmental Law Journal* fall symposium "Condemning Open Space," November 2, 2007.

Index